The Founding of the Swiss Military System, 1300–1400

The Battles of Morgarten, Laupen, Sempach, and Näfels

Albert Winkler

Helion & Company Limited
Unit 8 Amherst Business Centre
Budbrooke Road
Warwick
CV34 5WE
England
Tel. 01926 499 619
Email: info@helion.co.uk
Website: www.helion.co.uk
X (formerly Twitter): @Helionbooks
Facebook: @HelionBooks
Visit our blog https://helionbooks.wordpress.com/

Published by Helion & Company 2026
Designed and typeset by Mary Woolley, Battlefield Design (www.battlefield-design.co.uk)
Cover designed by Paul Hewitt, Battlefield Design (www.battlefield-design.co.uk)

ISBN 978-1-806720-66-8

British Library Cataloguing-in-Publication Data.
A catalogue record for this book is available from the British Library.

For details of other military history titles published by Helion & Company Limited contact the above address or visit our website: http://www.helion.co.uk.

We always welcome receiving book proposals from prospective authors.

Contents

Introduction

The late medieval Swiss military was among the first systems in Europe to invent advanced infantry tactics, largely in the fifteenth century. Using cutting-edge formations, impressive discipline, and effective weaponry, the Swiss innovations were instrumental in creating a true tactical infantry capable of aggressive action as well as strategic retreat. Before such modifications could be made, the Swiss had to establish a strong and able military capable of defending their lands and assuring their independence. These challenges were met largely in the fourteenth century. In a series of wars and battles that included Morgarten (1315), Laupen (1339), Sempach (1386), and Näfels (1388), the Swiss demonstrated their effectiveness and flexibility in manoeuvre, deployment, and combat which would lead to further advances and the maturing of their systems in the following century.

Political realities in the German Empire at the beginning of the fourteenth century were harsh, and communities that wanted to gain or maintain their autonomy had to deal with serious external threats. Most frequently, this meant that military success was essential for survival. Many forces vied for authority, influence, and domination over the regions that formed the Swiss Confederation, which later developed into the modern

The *Habichtsburg* or Hawk's Castle, the original castle of the Habsburg family, located in Aargau, Switzerland. (Freaktalius Wiki Creative Commons)

state of Switzerland. The largest threats to Swiss sovereignty in this period were factions of nobles, most importantly the house of Habsburg, who were expanding their control over the region. In one of the ironies of Swiss and Austrian history, the original possessions of the Habsburgs, the *Habichtsburg* or Hawk's Castle, was founded in the eleventh century in the Aargau region which later became a canton of modern Switzerland. From a relatively modest beginning, the Habsburgs developed into a regional powerhouse which threatened the existence and autonomy of many areas in what eventually became Switzerland.

By the early fourteenth century, the tiny cantons of Uri, Schwyz, and Unterwalden began working together for mutual support and protection. They were so small that all their land area combined would be about the same size as the modern county of Dorset in England. Yet much of this region was covered by high mountains as part of the Alps and therefore was unsuitable for cultivation. In reality, these cantons were little more than mountain valleys. These small states had been cooperating with each other for decades to resist outside forces, and their resolve to retain their autonomy was severely tested in 1315 when a large Habsburg army came to plunder and subjugate these cantons. The sovereignty of the Swiss republics was clearly at stake, and the significant victory in the Battle of Morgarten in 1315 meant that they would survive and continue to develop their own national expression.[1] This success might have kept the modern cantons of Switzerland from developing into little more than the nearby Austrian provinces of the Vorarlberg and Tyrol. The achievement at Morgarten was also significant in a social sense because it was an early victory of free peasants, which allowed them to keep their liberties and independence in the face of challenges from the feudal forces that attempted to control them.[2] The first part of this monograph will address the development of the early Swiss to 1315 and demonstrate how political and social realities led to war.

1 Morgarten has attracted much scholarly attention. Important studies include, Carl Amgwerd, 'Die Schlacht und das Schlachtfeld von Morgarten,' *Mitteilungen des Historischen Vereins des Kantons Schwyz* 49 (1951), pp.1–222; Bruno Meyer, 'Die Schlacht am Morgarten: Verlauf der Schlacht und Absichten der Parteien,' *Schweizerische Zeitschrift für Geschichte* 16 (1966), pp.129–179; and Wilhelm Sidler, *Die Schlacht am Morgarten* (Zürich: Orell Füßli, 1910).

2 Collections of primary sources on the battle include Theodor von Liebenau, (ed.) 'Berichte über die Schlacht am Morgarten,' *Mitteilungen des Historischen Vereins des Kantons Schwyz* 3 (1884), pp.1–86 hereafter cited as Liebenau 'Berichte,' and Wilhelm Oechsli, *Die Anfänge der Schweizerischen Eidgenossenschaft: zur sechsten Säkularfeier des ersten ewigen Bundes vom 1. August 1291* (Zürich: Ulrich & Co., 1891), pp.206*–219*. The * designates the page numbers of sources in the appendix.

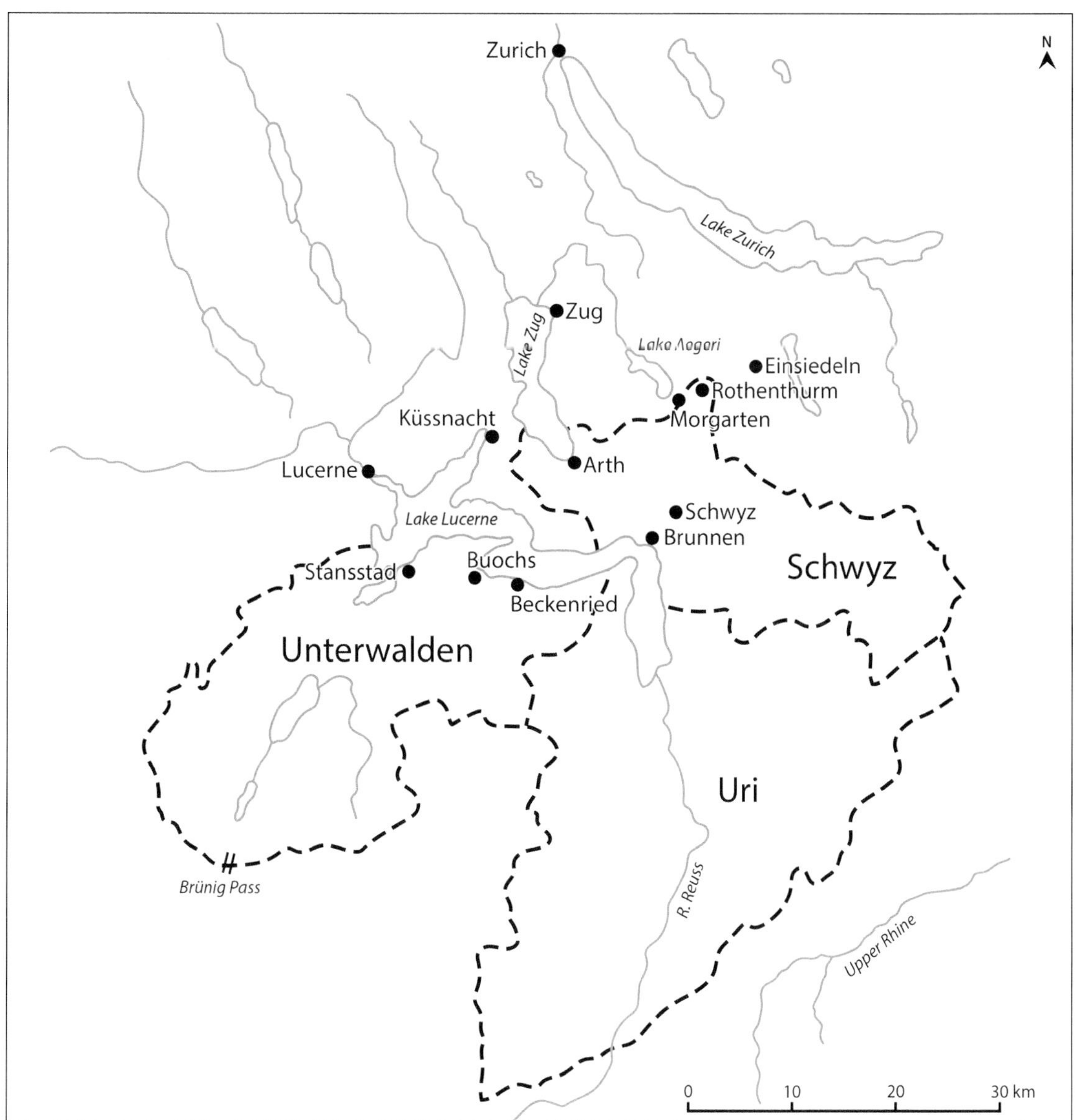

The Original Cantons

1

The Battle of Morgarten, 15 November 1315

Background to War

Uri, Schwyz, and Unterwalden were the first members of the Swiss Confederation. Often referred to as the 'Forest States' or 'Forest Cantons' (*Waldstätte*), these small communities were struggling for their autonomy as they faced external threats. During much of the late Middle Ages, Uri and Schwyz were part of the Zurich district over which the Habsburg family had authority. While the people of these states were largely free peasants and often chose their own leaders, the Habsburgs still held judicial powers over them and could arbitrate or pass judgement on their activities, especially dealing with foreign relations. A major step toward self-rule for the Swiss was the granting of charters of independence (*Freibrief* or *Freiheitsbrief*) for both Uri and Schwyz by the Hohenstaufen Emperors of Germany, Henry VII and Frederick II. Henry conferred this concession to Uri in 1231 and Frederick gave it to Schwyz in 1240. These endowments affirmed that the states were under the authority of the Emperor (*Reichsunmittelbar* or *Reichsfrei*) making them independent from the local feudal powers including the Habsburgs, but this sovereignty had to be put into practice, and many issues remained unresolved.[1] While Uri retained this status of autonomy, Schwyz and the Habsburg family engaged in a lengthy contest relating to judicial authority. Even though Schwyz controlled much of its domestic affairs, it still resented outside pressures, and it soon became the most militant power in resisting the Habsburg threat to the independence of the Forest Cantons.

1 Wilhelm Oechsli (ed.) *Quellenbuch zur Schweizergeschichte* (Zürich: Schulthess, 1918), pp.40–41.

In the 1420s more than a century after the events he described, the Bernese chronicler, Conrad Justinger, presented quaint details on the Habsburg oppression of the people of Schwyz. Justinger claimed the Habsburg overlords (*amtlüte*) placed over the peasants acted in a 'completely outrageous' (*gar frevenlich*) manner by abusing 'pious people, wives, daughters, and young women, and [the overlords] wanted to force their immoral desires [on them],' causing the people to rebel.[2] While this account certainly made the Schwyzers appear to be virtuous and innocent victims, Justinger clearly exaggerated. The communities of Schwyz commonly elected their own local leaders, and there were few if any Habsburg overseers nearby to abuse the people on such a personal level. Yet Justinger's account clearly underscored Schwyz's fear of the noble's use of arbitrary power.

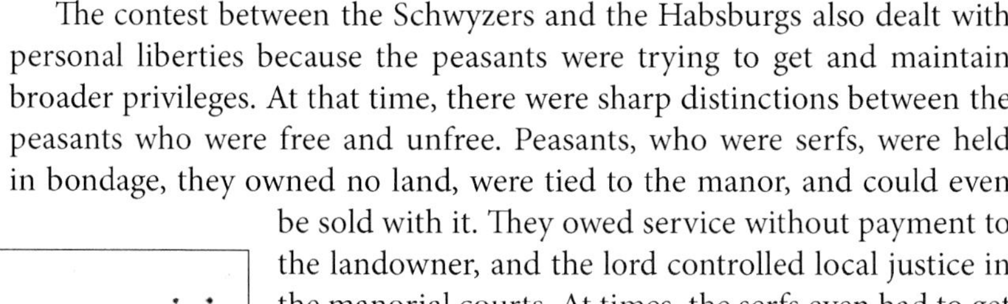

The contest between the Schwyzers and the Habsburgs also dealt with personal liberties because the peasants were trying to get and maintain broader privileges. At that time, there were sharp distinctions between the peasants who were free and unfree. Peasants, who were serfs, were held in bondage, they owned no land, were tied to the manor, and could even be sold with it. They owed service without payment to the landowner, and the lord controlled local justice in the manorial courts. At times, the serfs even had to get permission from the lord to cross bridges, use mills, bury family members, and to marry. Critically, the nobles held the right to provide military protection, and those in bondage could not perform this vital function. The authority to defend the state was a necessary step toward individual liberties and the independence of society and the state. In fact, the right to bear arms was often the most obvious privilege which separated the free from the unfree. These unrestricted peasants could also leave the service of the landowner and appeal to higher courts, thus circumventing local manorial justice to look for fairer judgements to their petitions.[3] The peasants coveted these rights, and those who enjoyed them wanted to keep and protect them from any threat.

Infantry from Uri defending the barricade. In the background, more soldiers from Uri are fighting with Austrian infantry. Bendicht Tschachtlan, Heinrich Dittlinger, *Tschachtlanchronik*, Bern, 1470. (Zentralbibliothek Zürich, Ms A 120)

2 Conrad Justinger, *Die Berner-Chronik* (Bern: Wyss, 1871), p.46. '*Ouch warent die amptlüte gar frevenlich gen fromen lüt, wiben, tochtern und jungfrowen, und wolten iren mutwillen mit gewalt triben, daz aber die erben lüte die lengen nit vertragen mochten; und sassten sich also wider die amptlüte.*' Justinger wrote near the year 1420. See also, Richard Feller and Edgar Bonjour, *Geschichtschreibung der Schweiz: vom Spätmittelalter zur Neuzeit* (Basel: Helbing & Lichtenhahn, 1979), pp.7–11.

3 Friedrich von Wyß, 'Die Freien Bauern, Freiämter, Freigerichte und die Vogteien der Ostschweiz im späteren Mittelalter,' *Zeitschrift für schweizerisches Recht* 18 (1873), pp.19–184 and Paul Schweizer, 'Die Freiheit der Schwyzer,' *Jahrbuch für Schweizerische Geschichte* 10 (1885), pp.2–25.

The people of Schwyz enjoyed more freedoms than those of the other Forest Cantons, but the residents of Uri also maintained many liberties even though some of them owed loyalty to local landowners and churchmen. The opening of the St. Gotthard Pass over the Alps, around 1236, made Uri an important station on a major trade route, and the community charged tolls and transportation fees, enhancing its wealth and importance. In contrast, much of the land in Unterwalden was owned by persons living outside the canton, and comparatively few free peasants lived there. While many of these people still owed service to lords and church estates, they were clearly agitating for liberties such as those enjoyed by their sister states nearby.[4]

The Habsburgs Encircle the Swiss

The Habsburg family tried to assert control over Schwyz and the other Forest Cantons by a policy of encirclement. One method was to control trade. Count Rudolf III von Habsburg, the Silent (*der Schweigsame*), who died in 1249, constructed the fortress of Neuhabsburg from 1241 to 1244 on the shores of Lake Lucerne on a prominence between Lucerne and Küssnacht to control commerce by that route. The Emperors Rudolf I von Habsburg, who reigned from 1273 to 1291, and his son, Albrecht I, who ruled from 1297 to 1307, followed the same policy. Wielding the combined power of the Habsburg faction and the Imperial prerogatives, they extended their influence on the approaches to the Forest Cantons by acquiring literally dozens of towns, areas, and courts by many means, including inheritance and purchase, thus effectively controlling access to the Forest States from the east, north, and west. Among the areas Rudolf gained was the city of Zug, from which the Habsburg army would march on Schwyz in 1315. Equally important was Albrecht's purchase of Interlaken in 1306 that was also an assembly point from which the Habsburgs launched their attack on Unterwalden at the same time as the invasion of Schwyz. Also significant was Rudolf's extension of control over the monastery of Einsiedeln in 1283.[5] The people of Schwyz and the Forest States took these threats very seriously, and they began a vigorous policy in 1293 of small-scale warfare to thwart Habsburg interests.[6]

The Forest Cantons also looked to each other for mutual support and protection both politically and militarily.[7] An undated document, written

4 Sidler, *Morgarten*, pp.32–41.

5 Sidler, *Morgarten*, pp.44 and 48–54.

6 Sidler, *Morgarten*, pp.114–115.

7 On the question of early treaties among the Forest States, see W. Oechsli, *Die Anfänge der Schweizerischen Eidgenossenschaft*; two works by Bruno Meyer, *Die Ältesten Eidgenössischen Bünde: Neue Untersuchungen über die Anfänge der Schweizerischen Eidgenossenschaft* (Zürich: Rentsch, 1938); and 'Die Entstehung der Eidgenossenschaft: Der Stand der heutigen Anschauungen,' *Schweizerische*

perhaps between 1244 and 1252, mentioned an agreement between Lucerne and the towns of Buochs and Stans, both in Unterwalden.[8] Pope Innocent IV wrote a letter on 28 August 1247 condemning a pact between Schwyz, Lucerne, and Sarnen, a town in Unterwalden. The Holy Father was supporting a plea by Count Rudolf III von Habsburg who claimed that he owned these areas, and the noble feared these places were operating autonomously. Innocent angrily criticised the agreement of the Swiss Cantons, because it aided Emperor Frederick II with whom the Pope was then at war.[9]

Swiss army during the siege operations. There are troops from Solothurn, Bern and Unterwalden present. Bendicht Tschachtlan, Heinrich Dittlinger, *Tschachtlanchronik*, Bern, 1470. (Zentralbibliothek Zürich, Ms A 120)

Future members of the Swiss Confederation entered into at least one agreement in 1291. Since the Federal Charter (*Bundesbrief*) of August 1291 may be a forgery,[10] the first authentic pact of that year was endorsed by Zurich, Uri, and Schwyz on 16 October 1291. These states designed the agreement to last three years, but it became invalid when the Habsburgs defeated Zurich in 1292, and the city had to come to terms with its adversaries, losing its ability to act independently.[11] Zurich later sent troops to support the Habsburg forces at the battle of Morgarten. Ironically, the best interest of the city in the long term rested with a victory of its adversaries in that engagement.

Zeitschrift für Geschichte 2 (1952), pp.153–205. See also Karl Meyer 'Der Ursprung der Eidgenossenschaft,' *Zeitschrift für schweizerische Geschichte* 21: 3(1941), pp.285–652.

8 J.E. Kopp, ed. *Urkunden zur Geschichte der eidgenössischen Bünde* (Lucern: Meyer, 1835), pp.2–3. Kopp reproduced the document and presented his case for its date in a footnote.

9 'Breve des Papstes Innocenz IV. gegen Schwyz, Sarnen und Luzern. Lyon 28 August 1247' as cited in Oechsli, *Quellenbuch*, pp.43–44. This is a translation of the document from Latin into German.

10 See Roger Sablonier, 'Schweizer Eidgenossenschaft im 15. Jahrhundert: Staatlichkeit, Politik und Selbstverständnis,' in *Die Entstehung der Schweiz: von Bundesbrief 1291 zur Nationalen Geschichtskultur des 20. Jahrhunderts* (Schwyz: Historischer Verein des Kantons Schwyz, 1999), pp.9–42. See also, Christoph Pfister, *Bern und die alten Eidgenossen: Die Entstehung der Schwyzer Eidgenossenschaft im Lichte der Geschichtskritick*, (Norderstedt: Dillum, 2006) and his 'Der Bundesbrief von 1291: Kritik einer Gefälschten Urkunde,' www.dillum.dh/html/bundesbrief_1291_kritik.htm Accessed 21 Nov. 2024.

11 'Rat und Bürger von Zürich schliessen mit Landammännern und Landleuten von Uri und Schwyz ein dreijähriges Bündnis, einer gegen jedermann zu helfen, 1291 Oktober 16.' *Urkundenbuch der Stadt und Landschaft Zürich* 6 (Zürich: Höhr, 1888–[1957]), pp.150–151. See also Oechsli, *Quellenbuch*, pp.49–50 and Anton Largiadèr, *Geschichte von Stadt und Landschaft Zürich* (Zürich: Rentsch, 1945), p.86.

Schwyz's Military Skill

Long before the Battle of Morgarten, the men of Schwyz demonstrated significant military ability, and the statements by early chroniclers that the Schwyzers were either 'defenceless' (*inermem*) or 'untrained at arms' (*armis inexercitatam*) in that engagement were way off the mark.[12] The Emperor Rudolf I hired mercenaries from that canton, and these troops participated in the Siege of Besançon in 1289. At that time, the men from Schwyz were 'accustomed to moving rapidly in the mountains,' and they dealt a decisive blow to the city defenders at Besançon in an impressive feat of arms by 'attacking down a mountain.'[13] The men of Schwyz again showed their skill in manoeuvring in steep terrain before the battle of Morgarten, and they also won that contest by an attack downhill. Rudolf was so impressed 'that the king [Rudolf] awarded them [the Schwyzers] a red banner of the Holy Roman Empire; that is all the emblems ... of the holy martyrs of our Lord Jesus Christ.'[14] This later became a red banner with a white Christian cross on it, which the Schwyzers and many other Swiss could carry in the future, and red and white later became the colours of the entire Swiss Nation.[15]

The Schwyzers' attacks on the monastery of Einsiedeln further demonstrated their martial abilities shortly before the Battle of Morgarten. A controversy over control of the monastery at Einsiedeln led to increased tensions between the Habsburgs and Schwyz because that noble family provided protection for the convent. In a 'boundary dispute' (*Marchenstreit*), Schwyz and Einsiedeln had contested the ownership of important lands since the tenth century, and the controversy was only solved much later in 1394 when Schwyz achieved formal control of the religious community. Before the final question of ownership was resolved, the people of Schwyz believed that much of the wealth of Einsiedeln belonged to them, which justified them taking the monastery's goods.[16]

In 1307, the Schwyzers launched a series of assaults on the cloister, and the official list of complaints (*Klagerodel*) about these raids, written by the monks in 1311, gave insights into how the men of Schwyz waged war. The troops of Schwyz broke into stalls and plundered storage facilities taking food, horses, and cattle, and they also killed a few monks while abusing others. Even though the attackers assaulted largely defenceless friars, the

12 The quotes are from Peter von Zittau and Johann von Victring respectively as cited in Liebenau, 'Berichte,' pp.23–24.

13 Mathias von Neuenburg, *Die Chronik des Mathias von Neuenburg*, Adolf Hofmeister, ed. (Berlin: Weidmann, 1955), p.41. '*soliti currere in montanis*' and '*descendentes montem irruerunt*.'

14 Justinger, *Berner-Chronik*, p.46. '*daz inen der küng gab an ir roten paner daz heilig rich, daz ist alle waffen ... der heiligen marter unseres herren Jesu Christi*.'

15 For an extensive work on Swiss flags see, A. and B. Bruckner, eds. *Schweizer Fahnenbuch*, (St. Gallen: Zollikofer, 1942).

16 Andreas Riggenbach, *Der Marchenstreit zwischen Schwyz und Einsiedeln und die Entstehung der Eidgenossenschaft* (Zürich: Fretz und Wasmuth, 1965).

Schwyzers deployed their forces with careful military efficiency, and they almost always came at night meaning they were able to march and deploy skilfully after dark. Of the 30 attacks listed, five involved 100 men, two included 200 men, and six contained 300 men. The men were under military leadership and came with banners flying. Two officers were often over each group of 100, and the overall leader of the state (*Landammann*) was frequently in charge of the raids. These numbers indicated the Schwyzers used tactical units of 100 men, but they also deployed smaller groups because the monks observed detachments of 20 and 30 men on one occasion. These smaller formations indicated a greater tactical flexibility because units of 100 could be cumbersome to deploy under various circumstances.[17]

Rudolf von Radegg, a monk at Einsiedeln, witnessed one of the most significant raids on the monastery on the night of 6/7 January 1314 and wrote an account of it. The men of Schwyz marched for hours on a route that took them past the mountain of Morgarten in the dark and cold of the winter's night. This force included some men on horseback and was the entire military strength of the canton. The men of Schwyz attacked at midnight and showed great military efficiency. They divided their forces and surrounded the religious community, making sure that no one could escape, and they advanced simultaneously to seize the monastery. The Schwyzers took much that was valuable, including books and cattle, and burned every document they could find, obviously hoping to destroy anything that might support the monks' claims to ownership of the land. Foreseeing this possibility, the abbot had hidden the most important manuscripts before the Schwyzers attacked, and these significant items survived. The troops took nine monks captive to Schwyz including Rudolf where they remained under the hospitality of a local priest until the Habsburgs negotiated their release 11 weeks later.[18] These prisoners were noblemen, and they were probably freed on the payment of a ransom.

Swiss polearm, circa 1380. (Metropolitan Museum of Art, New York)

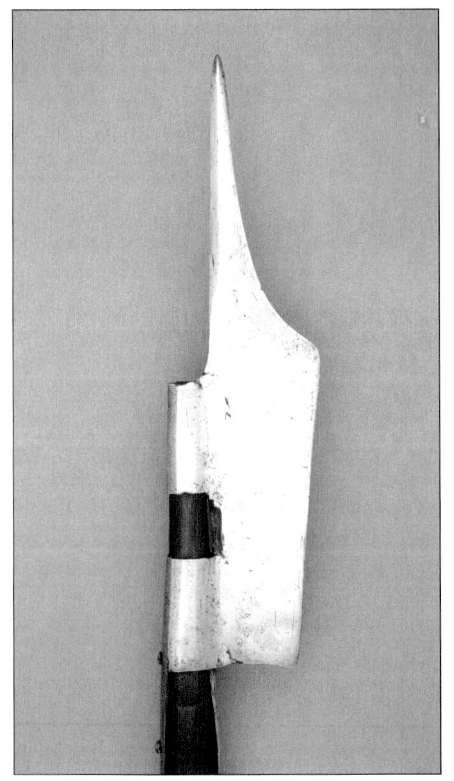

While attacking defenceless monks required little military skill, these actions provide valuable insights into the ability of the men of Schwyz to deploy before the Battle of Morgarten. The route from Schwyz to Einsiedeln led past the road going to Zug along the base of the Morgarten mountain. As was the case in 1315 when the troops deployed for the battle, it would have been easy for the Schwyzers to turn onto the road to Zug, follow it a short distance, and take positions

17 'Klagerodel: 1311, nach März 14–Juni 19,' *Der Geschichtsfreund: Mitteilungen des Historischen Vereins der fünf Orte Luzern, Uri, Schwyz, Underwalden Ob und Nid dem Wald und Zug* 43(1888), pp.345–359.

18 Rudolf von Radegg, 'Überfall Einsiedelns durch die Schwizer. 6/7 Januar 1314,' as cited in Oechsli, *Quellenbuch*, (1893), pp.261–273.

on the slopes of the hill. Equally significant, the men of Schwyz had shown they were skilled at coordinated efforts at night and in cold weather, which were essential abilities in their victory at Morgarten.

The attacks on Einsiedeln were clearly provocative to the Habsburgs, and this aggressiveness was part of Schwyz's foreign policy that led to war. The Schwyzers had also become more hostile to Einsiedeln because the attempts at arbitration had gone against them. Finally, Gerhard von Bevar (ruled 1307–1318), the Bishop of Constance, placed the interdict on Schwyz for its belligerence and for its refusal to pay compensation for damages. But these Church sanctions changed little politically, and the people of that canton were so outraged by the ban that the bishop's emissaries dared not read the official statement in Schwyz for fear of violence.[19]

Border Defences

The Schwyzers also prepared for hostilities by building border defences. Uri's location between the other two Forest Cantons left it largely invulnerable to direct assault, but Schwyz and Unterwalden were subject to invasion. The mountainous terrain restricted the avenue of approach to these two cantons, and their people secured various routes of possible attack by building border fortifications 'walls and trenches' called *Letzi*, from *letze* (border defence).[20]

The Schwyzers built these defences shortly before the battle. Most likely, they constructed the *Letzi* at Rothenthurm in 1310 to protect the route from Einsiedeln. Rudolf von Radegg mentioned the wall at Rothenthurm when he was taken captive to Schwyz in 1314. 'We came to the place where the defensive walls had been constructed.'[21] The fortifications there included a wall approximately 1 metre (3 feet) thick and 3 to 5 metres (10 to 16 feet) high. The barrier was about 400 to 450 metres (440 to 500 yards) wide, and it also supported two towers.[22] The Schwyzers built the defences at Brunnen about the same time because they were in place in 1315 before the battle. The walls were

Swiss polearm, circa 1380 (Metropolitan Museum of Art, New York).

19 Sidler, *Morgarten*, pp.62 and 115.

20 Stefan Sonderegger, 'Der Kampf an der Letzi: Zur Typologie des spätmittelalterlichen Abwehrkampfes im Bereich von voralpinen Landwehren,' *Revue internationale d'histoire militaire* 65 (1988), pp.77–78. The contemporary historian, Johannes von Winterthur also called them 'walls and trenches' '*muris et fossatis*' Johannes von Winterthur, *Johannis Vitodurani Chronicon: Die Chronik des Minoriten Johannes von Winterthur* Georg von Wyss ed. (Zürich: Höhr, 1856), p.71.

21 Rudolf von Radegg as cited in A. Nüscheler, 'Die Letzinen in der Schweiz,' *Mittheilungen der Antiquarischen Gesellschaft in Zürich* 18 (1872), p.13. '*Venimus, in quo sunt moenia structa, loco.*'

22 Jost Bürgi, 'Die Letzinen der Urkantone: ein Verteidigungssystem aus der Zeit der Bundesgründung,' *Mitteilungen des Historischen Vereins des Kantons Schwyz* 75 (1983): 35.

about 10 to 16 feet (3 to 5 metres) high and 3 feet (1 metre) wide. These barriers protected against potential attacks by land, but protections were built to guard against attacks by boat across Lake Lucerne. These defences included palisades, which were poles driven into the shores of the lake to block landings by water.[23]

The defences at Arth were among the most extensive. In 1314, the Schwyzers built two lines of barricades, in the lower part of the village (*Niederdorf*), and near Lake Zug to defend against any attacks by land or water. They also constructed palisades on the shores of the lake that were roughly 1,000 metres (1,100 yards) in length, and the walls on land were probably 2.5 kilometres (1.5 miles) long.[24] The barriers on land were described as being about 12 feet high (*12 Schuhe hoch*) or 3.66 metres and 3 feet thick (*3 Schuhe dick*) or 1 metre. They were well constructed out of stone and resembled the wall of a castle, complete with a trench 9 metres (30 feet) wide and 2 metres (6 feet) deep. They were dug along the front of the position to enhance its effectiveness. The tops of the walls were irregular in configuration and included merlons, which were solid positions for protection, and crenelations, that were the empty spaces between the merlons from which shots could be fired. At either end of these barricades, the natural obstacle of dense forests helped protect this position from flank attack. Believing in defence in depth, the Schwyzers also constructed another line of obstacles in the upper village (*Oberdorf*) of Arth at the same time.[25]

The people of Unterwalden also built defensive positions at this time, mostly to protect themselves from attack across Lake Lucerne. They constructed the extensive palisades and walls defending Stansstad, Buochs, and Beckenried about 1315, all on the shores of the lake.[26] These extensive fortifications constructed shortly before the Battle of Morgarten demonstrated that the people of Schwyz and Unterwalden, which were poor countries with small populations, made significant sacrifices in funds and effort to protect their lands from attack. Despite these impressive endeavours, the Schwyzers either overlooked an important avenue of approach or simply had too few resources to buttress it because they had failed to fortify the road leading from Lake Aegeri (Ägerisee) past the Morgarten Mountain into Schwyz. This oversight gave the Habsburg army a relatively unobstructed avenue of attack in 1315. The Schwyzers fortified this point of entrance at Hauptsee in 1322, seven years after the battle.[27]

23 Sidler, *Morgarten*, pp.117–118.
24 Sidler, *Morgarten*, p. [124] and Bürgi, 'Die Letzinen der Urkantone,' p.43.
25 Bürgi, 'Die Letzinen der Urkantone,' pp.39–48.
26 Nüscheler, 'Letzinen,' pp.7–17 and [61]. See also Sidler, *Morgarten*, pp.116–130.
27 Bürgi, 'Die Letzinen der Urkantone,' pp.29–55.

Swiss Manpower and Weapons

The military ability of the Forest Cantons was related to their manpower because strength was partially a function of the number of men available for service. The population of these cantons at that time cannot be determined precisely, but each likely contained several thousand persons at most. Certainly, no more than one quarter of the total population was an adult, physically fit male, and a reasonable estimate of the troop strength of Schwyz was 1,200 to 1,500 men. Military service began at age 16 and continued until the infirmities of old age precluded martial activities, usually by age 60. Young men were also considered legally adults at age 16.[28] The men of the Forest Cantons had no uniforms at this time, and they wore their usual peasant's clothing on campaigns. But they may have had white crosses sewn into their clothing, either the shirt or the pants or both, to distinguish them from their enemies.

There were hardly any social distinctions between the men in the army of Schwyz, because the community was comprised almost entirely of peasants, and few if any knights participated in the battle on their side. In his account of the battle, Justinger referred to groups of men he called *ächter* and *einunger* who fought for Schwyz. Some historians have assumed he meant men who were shock troops they called 'banished' (*Verbannten*), who led the Schwyzers into battle. These men were supposedly 'criminals' (*Verbrecher*) or 'convicts' (*Sträflinge*). This interpretation is an error derived from a misunderstanding of the terms *ächter* and *einunger* in Justinger's account, which seemed to refer to some kind of lawbreaker.[29] In fact, those terms indicated these men were not criminals but were the best, bravest, and most experienced troops available.[30] No doubt, such skilful warriors were placed in the most critical point in the battle.

Swiss army on the march. Diebold Schilling the Elder, *Spiezer Chronik*, approx. 1484/1485. (Bern. Burgerbibliothek, Mss.h.h.I.16)

The principal weapon wielded by the men of the Forest Cantons was the halberd, a variation of the battle axe, which had an iron axe blade with a sharp point on it similar to a spear point. Often there was also a hook on the side opposite to the axe blade. This iron accessory was attached to a wooden shaft 5 to 8 feet long (1.5 to 2.5 metres), and the weapon was light, versatile, and relatively inexpensive. The device was used for stabbing and slashing, and, when the hook was available, it could snag a knight's armour

28 Oechsli, *Quellenbuch*, p.230. All men of Schwyz aged '16 years and above' (*mansnamen xvi yarn alt und darob was*) served indicating this was the age of military obligation. Hans Fründ, *Die Chronik des Hans Fründ, Landschreiber zu Schwytz* Christian Immanuel Kind ed. (Chur: Gengel, 1875), p.48.

29 Justinger, *Die Berner-Chronik*, p.47.

30 'Die Verbannten' in Liebenau, 'Berichte,' pp.10–15 and Sidler, *Morgarten*, pp.182–184.

Swiss halberd, 1380–1430. (Metropolitan Museum of Art, New York)

and be used to pull him from his mount. Once on the ground, a heavily armoured cavalryman was out of his element and at a disadvantage. Johannes von Winterthur wrote that the Schwyzers had these 'very terrible' weapons with which they could cut up their heavily armoured enemies into pieces as though 'with a razor.'[31] The Schwyzers also wore shoes with iron spikes affixed to them that made deploying on the steep and slippery slopes of hills and mountains much easier giving them a considerable advantage over their enemies on foot and horseback who had no such devices.[32]

Some of the Swiss carried other weapons including daggers, but few if any had crossbows or other arms that could shoot projectiles, yet they often opened battle by throwing stones allowing them to do damage at a distance. The Habsburg knights on horseback and the foot soldiers who accompanied them wielded the typical weapons used by well-equipped armies at that time including swords, spears, and daggers. They also had defensive armament such as helmets, shields, and chain mail pants and shirts.[33] The Habsburg army was clearly formidable, and its troops were 'the strongest, best chosen, most battle experienced, most skilful, and most fearless [men].'[34]

The Habsburg Plan of Attack

The conflict between the Forest Cantons and the Habsburgs became part of a war for the throne of Germany. In 1313, the Emperor Henry VII died, and ambitious and powerful nobles soon vied for his position. Louis IV of Bavaria (Ludwig the Bavarian) won this contest and was elected to the throne in October 1314, but the Habsburg faction, led by Frederick I, the Handsome (*der Schöne*), disputed the election, and civil war ensued. Frederick's younger brother, Leopold, also known as Duke Leopold I of Austria (ca. 1290–1326), supported his sibling's candidacy, while the Forest

---

31 Johannes von Winterthur, *Chronik*, pp.37–72. '*Illo apellate helnbartam, valde terribilia, quibus adversarios firmissime armatos quasi cum novacula diviserunt et in frusta conciderunt.*'

32 Johannes von Winterthur, *Chronik*, p.72. '*Instrumentis pedicis et ferreis induit quibus faciliter gressum vel gradum in terra fixerant in montibus quantumcumque proclaims; inimicus et inimicorum equis minime pedes suos sistere valentibus.*'

33 Philipp Müller, 'Morgarten: ein Beitrag zur Waffentechnik,' *Mitteilungen des Historischen Vereins des Kantons Schwyz* 88 (1996), pp.23–40. Two works by Hugo Schneider also in the *Mitteilungen*, 'Die Bewaffnung zur Zeit der Schlacht am Morgarten,'58 (1965), pp.37–49 and 'Schwert und Dolch aus der Zeit der Schlacht am Morgarten, 1315' 57 (1964), pp.137–146.

34 Johannes von Winterthur, *Chronik*, p.71, '*miliciam robustissimam et electissimam et ad pungnandum peritissimam et intrepidissimam.*'

Cantons sought to weaken Habsburg influence by sustaining Louis. The campaigning between Louis and Frederick in 1315 was indecisive, but late in the year, Leopold decided to invade the Forest Cantons. Louis's supporters had already slowed their activities as winter approached, but there was still time for Leopold to wage a rapid campaign before the onset of harsh weather. A quick, decisive expedition against the Swiss would remove the threat from the Forest Cantons, and the subsequent plundering of their lands would provide needed food, supplies, and funds to help sustain the Habsburg war effort.[35] In fact as Duke Leopold's army advanced, his men carried 'ropes and cords' (*restes et funes*) with which to lead away captured cattle.[36]

Frederick and Leopold led a large army in the summer of 1315 believed to be 20,000 men on foot and 1,300 well-armed knights on horseback.[37] But a smaller force would actually attack the Forest Cantons. As allies of the Habsburg faction, contingents of men from Zurich, Lucerne, Zug, and Glarus accompanied them.[38] Each one of these states would later become valued members of the Swiss Confederation. In an irony of the situation, it was in the best interest of these states in the long run to be defeated at Morgarten. Victory seemed assured for Duke Leopold, if he could bring his impressive force to bear on the relatively small number of Swiss troops. The best hope the Forest Cantons had for success was to defeat the Habsburg army before it could be fully deployed against them.

Leopold I of Habsburg (Wiki Creative Commons)

Leopold divided his forces for a two-pronged attack on the Forest Cantons from opposite directions. Count Otto von Strassberg led one of these advances, and he assembled his force at Interlaken to strike at Unterwalden from the southwest over the Brünig Pass. On the same day, 15 November 1315, the Duke led another army to invade Schwyz from the north. Striking at the Forest Cantons from two directions at the same time seemed to be a good strategy because the Swiss would have difficulty meeting such threats. Yet the Swiss enjoyed interior lines of

35 Alois Niederstätter, *Die Herrschaft Österreich: Fürst und Land im Spätmittelalter* (Wien: Ueberreuter, 2001), pp.120–121.

36 Johannes von Winterthur, *Chronik*, p.71.

37 Johannes von Winterthur, *Chronik*, pp.70–71. '*circa mille trecentos equites galeatos vel ultra et circa XX milia peditum.*'

38 Justinger, *Die Berner-Chronik*, p.47.

Austrian infantry. Diebold Schilling the Elder, *Spiezer Chronik*, approx. 1484/1485. (Bern. Burgerbibliothek, Mss.h.h.I.16)

communication, which meant they could concentrate their forces on one army, and, if victorious, turn their attention to the other. The size of the force the Duke led against Schwyz was probably half the number of the two armies, and it included roughly 9,000 men on foot and on horseback. Among these were about 2,000 mounted knights.[39]

Fortunately, the badly outnumbered Schwyzers received reinforcements from their allies. Uri faced no immediate danger, since the enemy marched only directly on Unterwalden and Schwyz, so Uri sent troops to the other cantons. Unterwalden sent men to aid Schwyz as well, even though an army also advanced on them, believing the defence of Schwyz was critical. The contingents sent to Schwyz numbered 600, and these additional forces played a key role in the battle. The combined Swiss forces reportedly numbered 2,000 men.[40]

The Bernese chronicler, Conrad Justinger, told a quaint story about Leopold's plans which illustrated a potential problem with them. A court jester or fool (*narre*), later believed to be Kuony (Kuoni) von Stocken, accompanied the army, and Leopold asked how the plans pleased him. He answered, 'not well.' When asked to explain, the jester responded, 'because everyone has counselled on how you will go into the land. [but] no one has explained how you will return.'[41] This story was probably apocryphal, but it indicated a potential weakness in the Duke's plans because no one considered the possibility of failure and the potential need for escape.

The Swiss Plans

The Swiss planned to ambush the Habsburg army when it advanced, but a knowledge of when and where these forces would march was critical to that attempt. When Leopold assembled his troops at Zug on 14 November 1315, he had only two logical directions of approach into Schwyz. He could either advance along the shores of Lake Zug to attack the formidable defences at

39 Recent historians often accept the number of 9,000 men among whom were 2,000 knights. Sidler, *Morgarten*, p.153 and Hans Rudolf Kurz, *Schweizerschlachten*, (Bern: Francke, 1962), p.8.

40 Justinger, *Die Berner-Chronik* p.47 and Peter von Zittau '*fere duo millia pugnantium*,' as cited in Liebenau, 'Berichte,' p.23.

41 Justinger, *Die Berner-Chronik*, p.47. '*Nu waz ein narre in dem here, der wart gefraget wie im der rat geviele? Do sprach er, nit wol; do fragten si in: warumb im ir rate übel geviele? Do antwurt er und sprach: darumb daz ir alle geraten hand, wie ir in daz lant koment, es hat üwer keiner geraten, wa ir harwider uskoment*.'

Arth, or he could march past Lake Aegeri and use the unobstructed road that went along the slopes of the Morgarten Mountain. Clearly, the route past Morgarten was the easiest means of approach, and the Schwyzers may have failed to fortify that area hoping to lure any attacking army into using that avenue of march, but they had to be completely sure it was used. The early historians of the battle have suggested that an intermediary or a traitor gave the Swiss this vital information. Johannes von Winterthur mentioned the 'count of Toggenburg' (*de Toggenburg comitem*), identified as Friedrich von Toggenburg, was a mediator between Schwyz and Leopold in negotiations to reach some kind of agreement. This effort failed, but during the mediation, the Schwyzers learned by which direction the Habsburg army would advance.[42] Conrad Justinger stated that a nobleman named 'von hünenberg' shot an arrow over the fortifications towards the Swiss with a note attached to it which read, 'defend yourselves at Morgarten.'[43] This man, Hartman von Hünenberg, reportedly held the people of Schwyz in high esteem.

These stories seemed plausible, but they remained uncertain, and other explanations were also possible. Clearly, many men knew the route of march, and Leopold's army may have been unable to keep a secret, meaning that the intelligence might have leaked out by numerous sources. The Schwyzers also used reconnaissance to discern their enemy's movements. A man on horseback could cover many miles in a few hours, rapidly bringing vital information on the activities of the Habsburg army. As one chronicler asserted, the men of Schwyz learned of the enemy's approach by 'diligent scouting.'[44] These scouts encamped on the road that led past the Morgarten Mountain, and 'watched it [the passage] all day and night.'[45] The people of Schwyz established a ruse at Arth to fool Leopold into believing that their main forces were stationed at that fortified town. The people lit watch fires on the walls of Arth, and young boys and women remained on the barricades to give the impression that the walls were defended by a large number of men.[46]

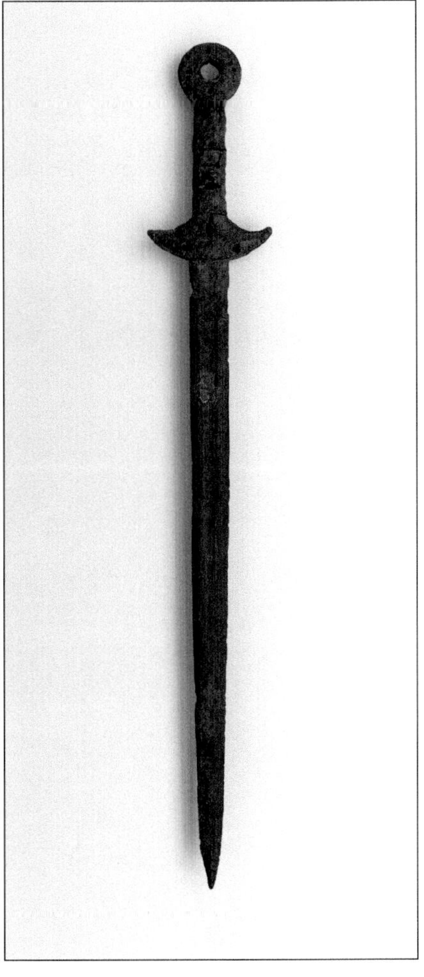

Swiss ring-pommel sword, early 1300s. (Metropolitan Museum of Art, New York)

42 Johannes von Winterthur, *Chronik*, p.72. '*Prescientes autem Switenses, per revelacionem comitis memorati, se in illa parte aggrendiendos.*'

43 Justinger, *Die Berner-Chronik*, p.47. '*hütend üch am morgarten.*'

44 Sebastian Seeman as cited in Liebenau, 'Berichte,' p.42. '*Speculatorium industria (qui tum forte ei in loco peccorum armenta a bestiarum raptu tuebantur) premoniti, in loco memorato Morgarte ei occurerunt.*'

45 Johannes von Winterthur, *Chronik*, p.72. '*Et erant custodientes ea tota die et nocte.*'

46 Peter Villiger as cited in Oechsli, *Die Anfänge*, p.217*. '*Allso hand sy von stundt an sich im ganzen land versamlet, sind den nächsten gegen den Morgarten gezogen und zu Arth die frowen lassen die wacht halten.*' See also, Rennward Cysat in Liebenau, 'Berichte,' p.72.

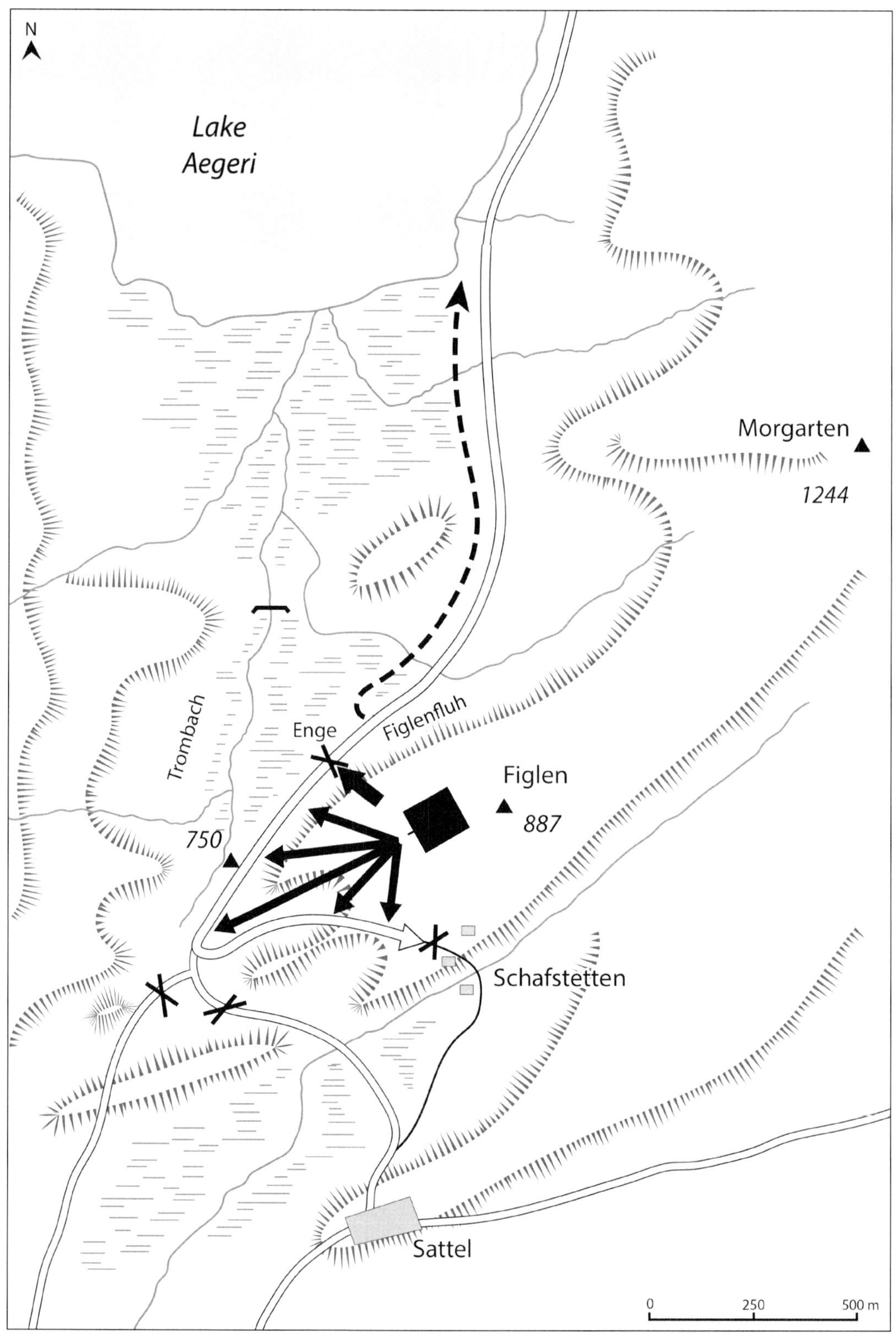

The Battle of Morgarten, 15 November 1315

While Schwyz's battle plans proved to be highly effective, the names of the leaders who made them remain uncertain. Konrad von Yberg of Schwyz led at least two of the attacks on the monastery of Einsiedeln, and Werner Stauffacher was the leader of the state (*Landamman*) in 1314, but the commanders for 1315, when the battle took place, were unrecorded. However, Stauffacher most likely led the men of Schwyz at Morgarten. The overall leader of Uri for 1315 was Werner von Attinghusen (Attinghausen) and the leaders of Unterwalden that year were Heinrich von Zubon (Zuben) and Klaus von Wizerlon (Wißerlon).[47]

The Battle

The Habsburg cavalry advanced ahead of the foot soldiers. The mounted knights were clearly the most formidable part of the army, and the impressive throw weight of a heavily armoured man charging on horseback was well known. The knights also had great disdain for the lower classes on foot. These noblemen likely believed they had a score to settle with the upstart peasants living in Schwyz, who had long resisted Habsburg domination. The road was perhaps only wide enough to accommodate two horses abreast, and the column of men on horseback could have stretched a few miles or kilometres along the road. The men on foot followed the advancing cavalry, and this procession could have also stretched for several miles or kilometres. Additionally, some of the troops came by boat across Lake Aegeri. One vessel from Aarow (Aarau) held 45 men.[48] The men of Schwyz and their allies wisely directed their attack at the knights at the front of the column. While the entire Habsburg army greatly outnumbered the Swiss, at the point of engagement, where the Schwyzers faced the knights, the numbers involved on both sides were about equal. Also, the attack on a mountain road meant that the knights were incapable of mounting a charge, meaning they had lost their main advantage in combat.

The Habsburg army marched on Schwyz early in the morning of 15 November 1315, and its progress was aided by the light of the moon that was only two days past full, but the brightness of the night also assisted the Swiss when they deployed to meet their adversaries. Leopold's advance was orderly and well planned despite one serious oversight. Apparently, he made no effort to reconnoitre the line of march to learn if there were any unforeseen obstacles on the avenue of approach. Perhaps in his overconfidence and arrogance, he thought this routine military precaution was unnecessary. Even a few men on horseback could have brought Leopold vital information that he was marching into an ambush, and the Duke soon

47 See 'Klagerodel,' *Der Geschichtsfreund*, pp.349–359 and letters to the leaders of Uri, Schwyz, and Unterwalden as cited in Oechsli, *Die Anfänge*, pp.197*–198* and pp.203*–204*.

48 Sprenger und Klingenberg as cited in Oechsli, *Die Anfänge*, pp.215*–216*.

Battle of Morgarten 15 November 1315. Bendicht Tschachtlan, Heinrich Dittlinger, *Tschachtlanchronik*, Bern, 1470. (Zentralbibliothek Zürich, Ms A 120)

learned a hard lesson about the grave risks of underestimating the Swiss.

The Schwyzers and their allies deployed on the uphill side of the road, which led past the Morgarten Mountain. These forces were spread out along this route, so they could strike a large section of the approaching column simultaneously. The Habsburg army marched along the road in the predawn light of morning, when the Swiss struck. In one of the earliest accounts of the action, the attackers, having allowed the Duke to advance into a trap, immediately 'sprang forward from the mountain just like mountain goats, throwing stones, killing most [of the defenders], who were in no way able to defend [themselves] or to escape.'[49]

The tactic of throwing stones at the beginning of an attack was often used by the Swiss early in their history, which was the case later in 1339 at the Battle of Laupen.[50] The stratagem of hurling stones was a crude form of fighting because the accuracy of thrown rocks was poor, and this tactic could only be used at very close range. Likely, the Schwyzers threw stones because they had few weapons capable of killing at a distance such as crossbows. The rocks thrown at Morgarten could have helped confuse the enemy and might have done some damage, but this barrage of stones was of short duration, and the Schwyzers soon advanced to meet their adversaries.

The Schwyzers attacked rapidly on the slippery slopes using their iron footgear for traction, and the Habsburg forces were caught completely out of their element. The initial attack swept through the knights so rapidly that they were unable to give any effective resistance. The Swiss advanced courageously from their hiding places and enclosed their enemies who were trapped 'just as fish in a net and [the Schwyzers] killed them without resistance [being offered].'[51] The observation that the Habsburg forces were ensnared in groups helps clarify how the Schwyzers and their allies fought the battle. Clearly, the Schwyzers enjoyed some tactical flexibility in their units of 100, 200, and 300 troops, and they may have used these sections to mass men at critical junctures to dissect Leopold's column. Once the line of knights was broken into sections, the Swiss easily surrounded these groups and destroyed them. These tactics made sense because they allowed the Swiss to keep in close proximity to each other, preserve unit cohesion, and maintain the ability to deploy for further action. If the Schwyzers and their

49 Johann von Victring as cited in Liebenau, 'Berichte,' p.24. '*Duci introitum concesserunt ... et quasi ibices de montibus scandentes labides miserunt, plurimos occiderunt, qui se defendere neque evadere ullo modo potuerunt.*' The account dates from 1340.

50 Justinger, *Die Berner-Chronik*, p.89.

51 Johannes von Winterthur, *Chronik*, p.72. '*Animati et valde cordati contra eos descendunt de latibulis suis et eos quasi pisces in sagena conclusos invadunt et sine omni resistencia occidunt.*'

allies were simply spread along the slopes, then the ability to redirect their activities would have been lost once the initial onrush had been made.

The Schwyzers used their halberds to cut down the knights, and they 'slew both lords and horses.'[52] As platforms from which the cavalrymen could fight, the mounts were also military targets. The Swiss so rapidly cut down their enemies that Johannes von Winterthur stated, 'It was not a battle but only ... a butchery.' Additionally, Duke Leopold's men were just like 'sacrificial animals brought to slaughter.' The Schwyzers spared no one, took no prisoners, and cut down their enemies 'without [class] distinction' (*indifferenter*).[53] Social divisions were often significant on the battlefields of Europe in this era because many of the knights were wealthy, and these men were often taken captive and held for ransom. In something like a gentleman's agreement, the upper classes were willing to take prisoners of their social equals hoping for the same treatment in return. This meant that combat was less dangerous for them than the men from the lower classes. By killing these knights without consideration of status or wealth, the Swiss made a social as well as a military statement.

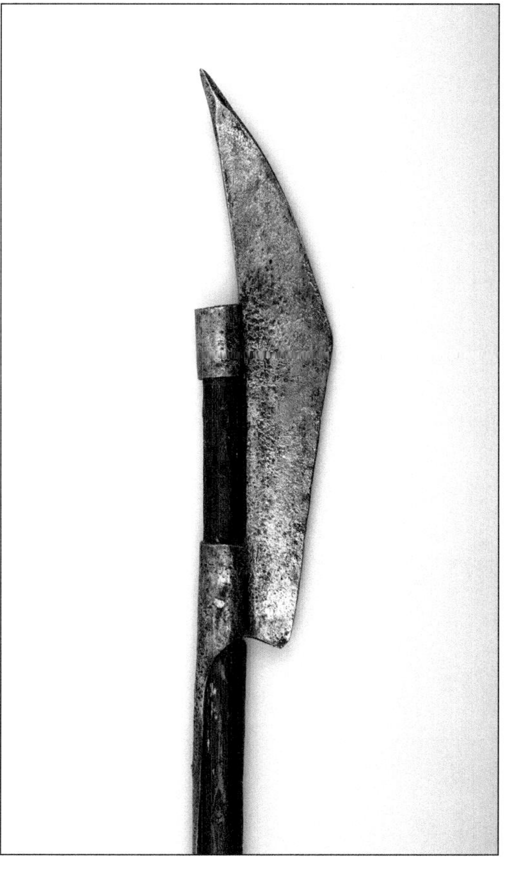

Swiss halberd, circa 1400 (Metropolitan Museum of Art, New York)

The Schwyzers and their allies directed the initial attack against the knights, the most-feared adversaries, but they also struck the men on foot. Pressing their advantage, the Swiss rolled up much of the Habsburg column by attacking down the line of marching men. Possibly, the Schwyzers also attacked the enemy infantry near the lake at the same time they overwhelmed the cavalry. Leopold's foot soldiers soon panicked, lost unit cohesion, and any semblance of resistance rapidly crumbled. Another factor in the loss of discipline among the infantry was the flight of the knights. When the Swiss attacked the nobles, many of these men turned to run away and trampled their own men killing many of them. 'When the servants of the Duke saw [the attack] they all turned back and fled from there. And the first one to flee was Count Hainrich [Heinrich] von Montfort, the canon, who killed many [of the Duke's] men [on foot] with [his] horses.'[54] Only the contingent of

52 Hans Gloggner's Zürcher Chronik as cited in Liebenau, 'Berichte,' p.34. '*Da warent switzer uf dem berg und sluogen herren und ross.*'

53 Johannes von Winterthur, *Chronik*, p.73. '*Non erat pungna se tantum ... . quasi mactatio.*'

54 *Zürich Chronik* (1428) as cited in Liebenau, 'Berichte,' p.32. '*Do das des hertzogen diener ersachent, do kartent si sich all umb, und fluchent dahin, und der erst der floch, der war graff Hainrich von Montfort, der corherr, der vil volks ertot mit den rossen.*' See also Heinrich Brennwald and Aegidius (Gilg) Tschudi as cited in

50 men from Zurich made the mistake of attempting to hold their position because they 'did not want to flee' (*woltend nit fliehen*), but their courage was misspent, and they were all killed in the onrush. Their bodies lay close together (*by einandren*) or were piled upon each other.[55] The foot soldiers at the front of the column suffered the heaviest casualties, and more men farther back survived. Only one man from the town of Winterthur died because he got separated from the other men and joined the nobles farther forward.[56]

Desperate to save themselves from the onslaught of their adversaries, the men in the Habsburg army tried to escape by retreating back up the road. At times, the fleeing men were so pressed together in their panic that 'they could neither defend themselves nor flee.'[57] The attack pushed many men into the lake where they drowned being weighed down by clothing and armour. Others jumped into the lake attempting to swim to the opposite shore and risked drowning rather than face the wrath of the Schwyzers.[58] The water in November was very cold, and the lake was one mile (1.5 kilometres) or more across, so few survived. The 45 men from Aarau, who came by boat, rushed to the vessel, but the craft sank under their weight, and they all drowned.[59]

While escape was difficult, many survived, including Duke Leopold, who evaded death because an aide saw an avenue of flight. 'The Duke, himself having been informed by one who had observed a path [to use to] get away, escaped with difficulty.' Leopold was fortunate, but his casualties were heavy. In fact, 'the flower of the army' (*flos militie*) had been killed.[60] 'From each community, castle, and town there were many men killed and because of that everywhere ... only the voice of crying and wailing was heard.'[61] The names of over 50 prominent nobles who fell in the battle were recorded in the Swiss books of remembrance (*Jahrzeitbücher*), but there may have been many more. Friedrich von Toggenburg, who may have warned the Schwyzers of the approach of Leopold's army, was among the dead.[62] The total number killed in the Habsburg Army was roughly 2,000

Liebenau, 'Berichte,' pp.47 and 63 respectively.

55 *Zürcher Chronik* (1449) as cited in Liebenau, 'Berichte,' p.35. See also, Gloggner as cited in Liebanau, p.34. '*Und verlurent die von zürich fünzig man.*'

56 Johannes von Winterthur, *Chronik*, p.73.

57 Victring, as cited in Liebenau, 'Berichte,' p.24. '*Qui se defendere neque evadere ullo modo potuerunt.*'

58 This is one of the best documented aspects of the battle, see Justinger, *Die Berner-Chronik*, p.48, Johannes von Winterthur, *Chronik*, p.73, and accounts by Stuhlmann, the *Zürcher Chronik*, Gloggner, and the Berner Königshofen as cited in Liebenau, 'Berichte,' pp.29, 33–34, and 37, respectively.

59 Joachim von Watt (Vadian) as cited in Liebenau, 'Berichte,' p.55.

60 Victring as cited in Liebenau, 'Berichte,' p.24. '*Dux ipse ex informatione cuiusdam, qui observabat semitas exitus, vix evasit.*'

61 Johannes von Winterthur, *Chronik*, p.73. '*De singulis civitatibus castellis et oppidis plures interempti fuerunt et ideo ubique ... sola vox fletus et ululatus audita est.*'

62 The books of remembrance are found in Liebenau, 'Berichte,' pp.81–85 and

men. Johannes von Winterthur stated that 1,500 had been killed by the sword, but he added that this number did not include those who drowned. Mathias von Neuenburg also wrote that 1,500 men had fallen, and Twinger von Königshofen stated that roughly 1,500 knights and their attendants, along with 500 infantry were also killed.[63]

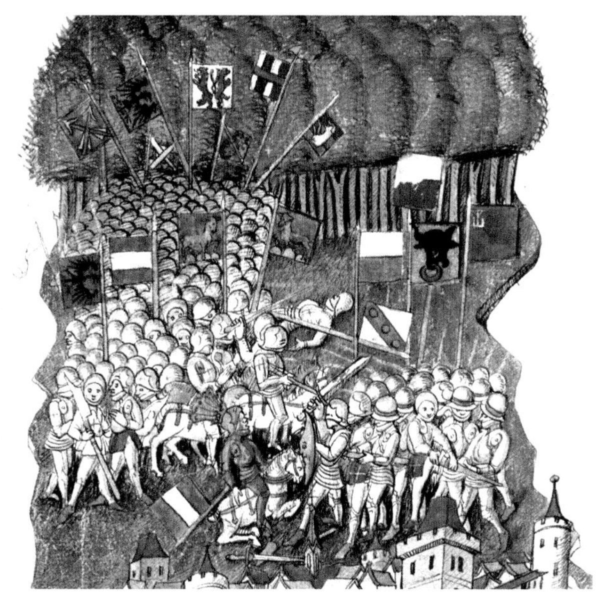

Swiss infantry in fight against Austrian cavalry and infantry. Bendicht Tschachtlan, Heinrich Dittlinger, *Tschachtlanchronik*, Bern, 1470. (Zentralbibliothek Zürich, Ms A 120)

In comparison, the Swiss losses were few. One erroneous source reported that the Schwyzers lost 'no more than one man.'[64] A careful modern study has stated that seven men from Schwyz lost their lives, while another seven men from the Uri and Unterwalden contingents were also killed.[65] The victory for the Swiss at Morgarten was such a lopsided contest that it may be considered among the greatest achievements in the entire history of warfare.

As a young boy in school, Johannes von Winterthur saw 'with my own eyes' (*occulis meis conspexi*) the men returning to Winterthur with some anxiety because he feared for the life of his father. Johannes finally saw his father, and, with great excitement, the boy ran to meet him in front of the city gate. The young scholar also saw Leopold return after the battle, and the Duke seemed understandably overcome with grief, worry, and exhaustion.[66]

While the Battle of Morgarten destroyed one Habsburg army, the other invasion force continued to advance on Unterwalden. The men of Schwyz, and the contingent from Unterwalden that had fought at Morgarten, left the battlefield rapidly to deploy against the remaining menace, but this effort was unnecessary. Otto von Strassberg and his men had skirmished insignificantly with enemy forces, but, when the leader received a glove or gauntlet turned inside out, he knew that Leopold's army had been defeated and immediately abandoned the campaign by withdrawing his troops.[67]

Oechsli, *Die Anfänge*, pp.217*–219*.

63 Johannes von Winterthur, Mathias von Neuenburg, and Twinger von Königshofen as cited in Liebenau, 'Berichte,' pp.210*–11*. Twinger stated 150 gleves (*anderhalp hundert glefen*) or 1,500 men had died.

64 *Zürcher Chronik* as cited in Liebenau, 'Berichte,' p.35. '*nit mer denn ain mann*'

65 Sidler, *Morgarten*, p.204.

66 Johannes von Winterthur, *Chronik*, p.73.

67 Justinger, *Die Berner-Chronik*, p.49. '*Ouch wart dem grafen von Strasberg ein letzer hentschuch gesent von den herren die am morgarten entrunnen, davi er verstund, daz si am strit verloren hatten.*'

But Otto was among the casualties of these engagements. He suffered some kind of internal wound (*lesus intrinsecus*) and soon died.[68]

Once all threats of invasion had turned back, the Schwyzers returned to the battlefield to plunder the enemy dead, no doubt gaining considerable wealth in the process. The victors took weapons and armour from the fallen men and horses, and they also retrieved corpses from the lake to take anything of value from them. This effort was so thorough that few artefacts relating to the engagement have been found on the battlefield. Scores of important nobles had been killed, and their relatives retrieved many of these bodies to inter them in family vaults.[69]

The War after Morgarten

Since the contest between the Swiss and the forces of Duke Leopold was only a part of a much wider conflict, the hostilities continued after Morgarten. However, the advantage had gone to the victors of the battle, and they soon went on the offensive striking late in 1315 and in the spring of 1316. The men of Unterwalden attacked Interlaken, and forces from Schwyz also struck at Glarus largely for plunder. The Swiss and the Habsburgs signed a series of armistices that ran from 1318 to 1323, which effectively brought the fighting between them to an end.[70] Frederick von Habsburg's bid for the throne of Germany ended at the battle of Mühldorf in 1322 when he was captured by his enemies. Among the conditions of his release in 1325 was the renunciation of Frederick's claim to the office of Emperor.[71]

On 9 December 1315, only 24 days after the Battle of Morgarten, representatives of the Forest Cantons concluded a defensive alliance at Brunnen in the state of Schwyz. The 'Brunnen Treaty' (*Brunnen Vertrag*) remains one of the most important agreements ever made among the Swiss. It bound the three cantons to cooperate on any military ventures, to come to one another's aid in time of emergencies, to guarantee peace among the signers, and to assure cooperation on all matters dealing with foreign powers. Significantly, this accord would 'remain eternally and continuously' (*ewig und stete beliben*) binding on the states, and it is still in force today.[72] While the authenticity of the Federal Charter of 1291 may be in question, the Brunnen Treaty is certainly genuine. Although the existence of the Federal Charter was unknown until the eighteenth century, the Brunnen Treaty has been remembered since it was signed, and it may be the oldest authentic agreement of an 'eternal' nature among the Swiss. With the creation of a

68 Matthias von Neuenburg as cited in Liebenau, 'Berichte,' p.28.

69 Johannes von Winterthur, *Chronik*, pp.73–74.

70 Sidler, *Morgarten*, pp.216–219.

71 Niederstätter, *Die Herrschaft Österreich*, pp.122–128.

72 Oechsli, *Quellenbuch*, pp.64–66.

treaty binding the Forest Cantons and other members who soon joined, the pact may well be considered the Swiss Confederation at that point.

The victory at Morgarten made the Brunnen Treaty possible because the viability of cooperation among the Forest Cantons had been clearly confirmed. These cantons, held together by the Brunnen Treaty of 1315 and later alliances, maintained the viability of the Confederation allowing it eventually to evolve into the modern Swiss nation. In a stunning feat of arms at Morgarten, the free Swiss peasants defeated a competent feudal army led by mounted knights in one of the most lopsided battles in history. This victory was among the first of its kind, and it signalled the development of infantries and the decline of cavalries in the armies of Europe. Over the next two centuries, the Swiss would continually demonstrate how free men could protect themselves and secure their privileges by their military prowess.

2

Morgarten and the Founding of the Swiss Confederation

The 'Federal Charter' or *Bundesbrief* of 1291 has often been cited as the document which founded the Swiss Confederation, but the victory at Morgarten and the following Brunnen Treaty of 1315 are more authentic and important, and they should be regarded as the beginnings of the Swiss state. The Federal Charter has long perplexed scholars who have tried to understand its structure, wording, and historical impact, and many issues remain unresolved. These problems have led many historians to believe it is a forgery.[1]

The text of the Federal Charter is 17 lines long, and the manuscript is written on a piece of parchment that is approximately 8.25 inches high (209 to 210 millimetres) and about 12.6 inches wide (318 to 321 millimetres).[2] The item is in Latin and includes 469 words, but 304 of the words have been shortened by deleting letters. The document was written using contractions, superscripts, shorthand signs, abbreviations, and dashes, which were common devices employed by scribes at the time. However, the document's scribe is unknown, and the item was written in a script and uses abbreviations unknown anywhere else.[3]

The document stated that in view of the dangers of the time, each canton agreed to come to the aid of the others in the face of all possible internal and external threats no matter what the expense in people and goods. This pact

1 The classic account of the establishment of the Swiss Confederation is Wilhelm Oechsli, *Die Anfänge*. See also the compilation of essays in Josef Wiget, (ed.) *Die Entstehung der Schweiz: von Bundesbrief 1291 zur Nationalen Geschichtskultur des 20. Jahrhunderts* (Schwyz: Satz, Druck und Repros, 1999).

2 Walther ab Hohlenstein, *Urschweizer Bundesbrief 1291: Untersuchungen zur Immanenten Bestimmung seines Zeugnisses* (St. Gallen: Schloss Schwarzenbach, 1956), pp.11–13 and 60.

3 Pascal Ladner, 'Urkundenkritische Bemerkungen zum Bundesbrief von 1291,' in *Die Entstehung*, pp.105–108.

renewed the ancient form of the league which was also established by oath.[4] The states agreed to allow no foreign or unfree judges to have authority over them. But, when disputes arise, the most prudent members of the alliance would adjudicate them, and all the members of the pact would support and uphold the Judgements made. Murderers should be executed, and anyone damaging the possession of others must pay restitution. The stated agreements will 'endure forever' (*in perpetuum duraturis*), and the document is dated 1291 'at the beginning of the month of August' (*primo incipiente mense Augusto*).

The Federal Charter certainly was no constitution that created a new state. It was simple and direct, and it explained the nature of an alliance, but it has many curious aspects that have long puzzled historians, and some are so perplexing they may be unresolvable. The document seems to have been composed in haste, and the item appears to be pieced together from four sources.[5] The Latin is quite obscure, and there are grammatical errors in it indicating it was written 'by a clumsy scribe.'[6]

Most of the text was written in the objective form (indirect discourse), which meant that the author wrote in the third person. However, the phraseology later shifts unexpectedly to the first person plural. Then, the wording returned to the objective form 'he shall be' (*fuerit*) where the grammatical voice remained for the rest of the document.[7]

Swiss trumpeters during the battle. Diebold Schilling the Younger, *Eidgenössische Chronik des Luzerners*, Lucerne, 1513 (ZHB Luzern Sondersammlung, S 23 fol.)

While each of the participating cantons, Uri, Schwyz, and Nidwalden (part of Unterwalden) should have received its own copy of the agreement, only one now exists, and it is located in the *Bundesbriefmuseum* (Federal Charter Museum) in Schwyz.[8] At that time, official seals were placed on documents to validate them, and each of the three Forest Cantons should have placed seals on the Charter. Uri's insignia is correct, but the seal of Schwyz

4 Anton Castell, *Die Bundesbriefe zu Schwyz: Volkstümliche Darstellung wichtiger Urkunden Eidgenössischer Frühzeit* (Einsiedeln: Benziger, 1969), pp.36–41. For translations into English, French, Italian, Romansh and German, see www.lexilogos.com/declaration/suisse_pacte_tableau.htm Accessed 17 Nov. 2004.

5 Pascal Ladner, 'Urkundenkritische Bemerkungen,' in *Entstehung*, pp.118–119.

6 Léon Kern, 'Notes: pour servir à un débat sur le pacte de 1291,' *Zeitschrift für schweizerische Geschichte*, 9 (1929), pp.340–346. '*Cet acte a été écrit par un scribe malhabile qui commis plusieurs fautes.*'

7 H[arry] Bresslau, 'Das älteste Bündnis der Schweizer Urkantone,' *Jahrbuch für schweizerische Geschichte* 20 (1895), pp.29–32.

8 Roger Sablonier, *Gründungszeit ohne Eidgenossen: Politik und Gesellschaft in der Innerschweiz um 1300* (Baden: hier + jetzt, 2008), pp.163 and165–166.

is missing, and the wax symbol for Nidwalden is erroneous, because it is the seal of Obwalden.

No source exists on the creation of the Federal Charter including how, why, and by whom the pact was negotiated. The men who made the agreement were not listed in the source, and the document was unsigned. The date on the document 'at the beginning of August' (*incipiente mense augusto*), which was interpreted as 1 August in the nineteenth century, was also strange because a more specific date would be expected on a document north of the Alps. Breaking the month into parts such as 'at the beginning' or 'at the end' were expressions that were used in manuscripts in Italy at that time, while exact dates were used in the German Empire and in the Forest Cantons. In view of all these problems, the question of the authenticity of the document 'must be earnestly addressed.'[9]

The radiocarbon dating method has been used to date the parchment on which the Federal Charter was written. With a certainty of 68 percent, the goat or sheep from which the parchment was made died between the years 1265 and 1295. There was an 85 percent chance that the material was created between 1252 and 1312. Yet there was a 15 percent probability that the goat or sheepskin dated from 1352 to 1385.[10] However, the date of this material may still differ from that of the source's contents. The parchment could have been clipped from another document, and the text could have been added later. The fact that the manuscript has relatively narrow margins, especially on the right and left sides, could be evidence that the material was cut from another larger piece of parchment.

The importance of the Federal Charter on medieval Swiss history was minimal because the manuscript was either ignored or forgotten, even if it did exist. On 9 December 1315, shortly after the battle of Morgarten, the Forest Cantons concluded an agreement known as the Brunnen Treaty. This source is written in German for all to understand, and it stated for whom it was intended. 'Therefore, we announce and disclose to the fellow countrymen of Uri, Schwyz, and Unterwalden to all those who read this letter or hear it read that … '[11] It referred to no earlier agreements, including the Federal Charter, which could hardly have been the model for this alliance. The seals of Uri, Schwyz, and Unterwalden are affixed to it, and the document is clearly authentic. The treaty bound the three states to cooperate on any military ventures, to come to one another's aid in times of emergencies, to guarantee peace among the signers, and to assure cooperation on all matters dealing with foreign powers. Significantly, this accord would 'remain eternally and continuously' (*ewig und stete beliben*)

---

9 Sablonier, 'Der Bundesbrief von 1291: eine Falschung?,' in *Entstehung*, p.145.

10 Willy Woelfli and Georges Bonani, 'Datierung des Bundesbriefs mit der Radiokarbonmethode,' in *Entstehung*, pp.121–126.

11 For a copy in the original Medieval German see, Hohlenstein, *Urschweizer Bundesbrief*, pp.19–22. For a modern German translation see, 'Der Dreiländerbund. Brunnen, 9 Dezember 1315,' in Oechsli, *Quellenbuch*, pp.64–66.

binding on the cantons, and it is still valid today. As such, it may be considered the founding document of the Swiss state.[12]

In the following decades, new members became part of the Three States' Pact. Lucerne joined in 1332, Zurich became a member in 1351, both Zug and Glarus were in the agreement in 1352, and Bern was part of the coalition starting in 1353. None of these agreements refer to the Federal Charter of 1291, but each treaty was a milestone in the development of the Swiss nation.[13]

Early historians of the Swiss Confederation also ignored the Federal Charter or did not know of its existence. Centuries later, the document was finally 'discovered' either in 1758 or 1759.[14] While the Charter had become known at that point, it had little immediate impact on the writing of Swiss history. Later, important historians were divided in their opinions on the Federal Charter including Johannes Dierauer and Karl Dändliker who both wrote impressive multi-volume histories of Switzerland late in the nineteenth century. Dierauer stated that the Federal Charter created an 'eternal pact' and 'laid through this deed, the first foundation of the Swiss Confederation.'[15] Dändliker was more sceptical about the importance of the Federal Charter, and he wrote that the year 1291 was 'uncertain' (*unsicher*) in its importance, but 1315 was 'significant' (*gesichert*). He concluded that, 'the battle at Morgarten and the eternal pact of Brunnen 1315 have authenticated the existence of the [Swiss] Confederation.'[16]

Troops from Bern on the march. Bendicht Tschachtlan, Heinrich Dittlinger, *Tschachtlanchronik*, Bern, 1470 (Zentralbibliothek Zürich, Ms A 120)

The Federal Charter of 1291 was elevated to the founding document of Switzerland not by a consensus of the Swiss people or of Swiss historians

12 Roger Sablonier, '1315–ein weiteres Gründungsjahr der Eidgenossenschaft? Der Bundesbrief von 1315' *Der Geschichtsfreund: Mitteilungen des historischen Vereins Zentralschweiz* 160 (2007), pp.9–24.

13 Oechsli, *Quellenbuch*, 'Der Luzerner Bund. Luzern, 7. Nov. 1332,' pp.81–83; 'Der Zürcher Bund. Zürich, 1. Mai 1351,' pp.97–102; 'Aus dem Glarner Bund, 4. Juni 1352,' pp.104–106; 'Der Zuger Bund. Luzern, 27. Juni 1352,' p.106; and 'Der Berner Bund. Luzern, 6 März 1353,' pp.107–110.

14 Johann Heinrich Gleser, *Specimen observationum ex iure gentium et iure publico circa Helvetiorum foedera* (Basilaeae: Rudolfum Im-Hof, 1760). See also, Marc Sieber, 'Johann Heinrich Gleser (1734–1773) und die Wiederentdeckung des Bundesbriefs von 1291,' *Basler Zeitschrift für Geschichte und Altertumskunde* 91 (1991), pp.107–128 and Sablonier, 'Das neue Bundesbriefmuseum,' in *Entstehung*, p.172.

15 Johannes Dierauer, *Geschichte der schweizerischen Eidgenossenschaft* 5 vols. 1 (Gotha: Perthes, 1887–1917), p.92. '*Legten durch diese Tat den ersten Grund zur schweizerischen Eidgenossenschaft.*'

16 Karl Dändliker, *Geschichte der Schweiz mit besonderer Rücksicht auf die Entwicklung des Verfassungs- und Kulturlebens von den ältesten Zeiten bis zur Gegenwart* 3 vols. 4th ed. 1 (Zürich: Schulthess, 1900), p.426. '*Die Schlacht am Morgarten und der ewige Bund von Brunnen 1315 haben den Bestand der Eidgenossenschaft besiegelt.*'

but by an act of the federal government that was looking for a day of national celebration. On 5 November 1889, the seven members of the Federal Council (*Bundesrat*) gave a mandate to the Departments of the Interior and of the Military to write a report on a national holiday. These agencies presented their report on 21 November, stating that the Swiss Confederation began on 1 August 1291 with the Federal Charter, and the Federal Council announced that a national celebration would be held on 1 August 1891.[17] Elevating the year 1291 to the founding date of the Swiss Confederation meant that the nation could have its 600-year celebration in 1891 and would not have to wait until 1915 for a much better date.

The Swiss press soon responded to the mandated national holiday. The *Winterthurer Landbote* stated that in the 'mind and consciousness' (*Gemüth und Bewusstsein*) of the Swiss people, 1 August 1291 did not exist as the date of the founding of the state. The *Züricher Post* argued that 1 August 1291 had no place in the mentality of the modern Swiss and was also completely unknown to 99 percent of former generations.[18]

Criticism from historians on the use of the Federal Charter as the founding document of the Swiss state has increased over the years. One eminent scholar has stated, 'the so-called founding of the Swiss Confederation in 1291 ... is a figure of political discourse and not of historical argumentation.'[19] In view of all these problems and misgivings, the importance of the Federal Charter as the founding document of the Swiss Confederation must remain highly questionable, and the Brunnen Treaty of 1315, which was made possible by the victory at Morgarten is clearly much more important.

17 Georg Kreis, 'Der Mythos von 1291: Zur Entstehung des schweizerischen Nationalfeiertags,' in *Entstehung*, p.62.

18 *Thurgauer Wochen-Zeitung*, *Winterthurer Lindoe*, and *Zürcher Post* as cited in Kreis 'Mythos,' in *Entstehung*, pp.63–64.

19 Sablonier, 'Schweizer Eidgenossenschaft im 15. Jahrhundert: Staatlichkeit, Politik und Selbstverständnis,' in *Entstehung*, p.34. '*Die sogenannte eidgenönssische Staatsgündung von 1291 ... ist eine Figur des politischen Diskurses, nicht der historischen Argumentation.*'

3

The Expansion of the Swiss Confederation

Lucerne joins the Confederation 1332

While the victory of the Swiss peasants at Morgarten was highly significant militarily, socially, and politically, the battle left many issues dealing with the threat posed by the Habsburgs unresolved. In fact, that Austrian noble family sought revenge against the members of the Swiss Confederation, and the victory of Morgarten may be seen as an opening round of a protracted contest. These animosities and conflicts would last for nearly a century, only to be revived again a century later in 1499 with the Swabian War, and the outcome of these contests would only be determined by the efforts of many generations. To prevail, the Swiss would have to demonstrate their military skill many times and attract allies in that effort.

The Battle of Morgarten clearly demonstrated that the Swiss were able troops who could deploy at night and bring their enemies to battle on their own terms, but this success had its limitations, because the Confederates had chosen the terrain. To expand their power and to defend their borders adequately, these mountain ambushers had to develop the ability to take the fight to lower ground where the topography gave them fewer advantages. They also needed additional allies to strengthen their numbers and to prove their ability to fight in different environments. The success of the Swiss at Morgarten soon attracted attention by the areas nearby who also felt threatened by the Habsburgs and other factions of nobles.

Among these was the city of Lucerne. The town on Lake Lucerne was in an enviable position economically because the commerce flowing over the St. Gotthard Pass crossed the lake. The pass had been little used for centuries because of the steep terrain, but it was opened to commerce about 1220 with the construction of a bridge, known as the Devil's Bridge, over the precarious and very formidable Schöllenen Gorge near the headwaters of the Reuss River high in the Alps. This was a main trade route over the

Document confirming sale of Lucerne and surrounding area to King Rudolf I. It was sold by Murbach Abbey. (Staatsarchiv Luzern, StALU URK 488/8681)

Alps from Italy to the German Empire, which followed the Reuss River into the Uri Canton. The people of Uri became known as those who helped the trains of pack animals, mostly mules, carry their goods through their area. Once the caravans reached Lake Lucerne, the commodities of the pack trains were routinely transferred to boats to cross the lake to the city of Lucerne. This meant that Lucerne became an important link in transportation to provide boats and landing areas for goods to be taken further into the German Empire.

The Habsburgs recognised Lucerne's economic importance and sought to control the city. Facing the pressure of the Austrian noble house, Lucerne realised it needed allies to maintain its political and economic independence. The town on Lake Lucerne felt threatened by the nobles and Habsburgs as had the Forest Cantons, and the city was attracted by the military success of their new allies. Lucerne formally joined the Confederation in 1332. More than a century later Lucerne would be considered as part of the Forest Cantons, but throughout the fourteenth century, Lucerne was considered as being separate from the other original members of the Swiss Confederation. As a new and permanent member of the coalition, Lucerne was expected to follow similar military rules as the original members, and the numbers of men available for service in that state were increased. The geographic location of Lucerne also had certain advantages. Each one of the original members of the alliance bordered on Lake Lucerne, and with the addition of the new canton, the Confederation then fully encircled that body of water. Consequently, the cantons need not fear an economic blockade to prohibit commerce on the lake, and they no longer needed to build and maintain harbour defences. Also, trade and communication between them on the lake were enhanced and made more secure.

While the addition of Lucerne showed that the pact was attractive to at least one state in the short run, the coalition still controlled only a small geographic area and remained relatively weak. The addition of larger states with greater economic influence, more extensive land holdings, and a larger population would clearly enhance the viability of the alliance and aid in its chances of survival. The addition of Zurich and Bern would be most valuable in all these areas.[1]

Bern's Importance

In the late Middle Ages, Bern would eventually include a large area with a relatively substantial population, and it was an important state militarily from its very foundation. In 1191, Duke Berchtold V von Zähringen (1160–1218) established Bern as a military fortress to help meet the threat from the various noble factions in the area including the Austrians and the 'Burgundians,' now located in the Franche-Comté region of France which borders modern Switzerland. Berchtold placed the town on an advantageous position at a steep bend in the wide Aare River that was designed to be very defensible.[2]

There are a number of theories on how Bern got its name. An early chronicler of Bern, Conrad Justinger, presented a quaint story. 'He [Berchtold] wanted to name the city after the first animal to be captured in the forest. Soon a bear was the first to be captured. That is why the city was named Bern.'[3] The bear was the symbol of the city starting at least from the early thirteenth century.

Troops from Bern on the attack. Diebold Schilling the Elder, *Spiezer Chronik*, approx. 1484/1485. (Bern. Burgerbibliothek, Mss.h.h.I.16)

The bend of the river where Bern had been established was so sharp that it formed a peninsula, and as the fortress grew, the town walls were simply constructed farther and farther up the isthmus. The main weakness of the position was the fact that the surrounding area, particularly on the opposite side of the river, was high, and any besieging force could look down upon the city. The high ground was a good place to deploy such devices as catapults and trebuchets to throw stones into the town. When gunpowder came into use in the late fourteenth century, artillery could also be used to assault the city.

1 Dändliker, *Geschichte der Schweiz,* vol. 1, pp.474–482.

2 Kurz, *Schweizerschlachten,* p.17 and Emil Frey, *Kriegstaten der Schweizer: dem Volk erzählt* (Neuenburg: Bahn, [1904]), p.28.

3 Justinger, *Die Berner-Chronik,* p.8. *'Er* [Berchtold] *wolte die stat nennen nach dem ersten tiere so in dem walde gevangen wurd. Nu wart des ersten ein ber gevangen, darumb wart die stat bern genempt.'*

Bern would serve as a very important position to defend the property of the landowners of the area who enjoyed many privileges, yet it was very doubtful that the Duke intended to establish the city as a refuge for free workers. What he wanted, above all, was a solid military organisation among the new settlers, and it was obvious that service in a militia was an essential condition for anyone immigrating into the new town. Among the founding charters of Bern was a statement similar to what Berchtold V's father, Berchtold IV (ca. 1125–1186) issued to Freiburg im Breisgau a few years before. 'Whoever violates and does not obey, without a valid excuse, the call to an immediate [military] expedition will suffer the destruction of his house to the ground.'[4]

When Berchtold V died in 1218, the male line of the Zähringer family died out. At that time, the German Emperor Frederick II (1194–1250) declared that all possessions which that defunct lineage had held in the name of the Empire reverted back to the original owners. This meant that such towns as Bern, Zurich, Solothurn, Laupen, Gümmenen, and Murten were made Imperial cities and technically under the authority of the Emperor. But he was frequently far away and involved in other serious matters including the many threats to his Empire, and he was unable or unwilling to assert control over these towns and areas thus creating a power vacuum. In a practical sense, these cities were then virtually independent and free to follow their own policies.

Inevitably, the loss of Imperial power left many issues unsettled and led to numerous feuds and conflicts in the locality. This regional instability allowed Bern to start to spread its own power, influence, and control over many areas nearby. Bern used several means of expansion including inheritance, intimidation, purchase, and war. For over a century, Bern prevailed in numerous military contests, and it brought many peasant communities and fortresses under its control and influence. Its expansion was so successful and so unusual that it was nearly unique among German and Swiss lands in that era.[5]

Bern's Government

Bern advanced quickly using bold power politics that was supported by a strong aristocracy and a courageous citizenry sustained by effective means of government. The organisation of the Bernese political control in the thirteenth century was fairly complicated. On the top of the political structure was the mayor or *scultetus*, who had many responsibilities. He had judicial authority and served as the judge of the city or *judex urbis* and was elected yearly at Easter. He also sat as the chief minister over the city's

4 Frey, *Kriegstaten der Schweizer*, p.38.
5 Frey, *Kriegstaten der Schweizer*, p.38.

administrative councils, but most importantly, he served as commander of all the state's forces in the time of war.[6]

Under the mayor stood the 'Council of 12,' also known as the 'Small Council,' which was functioning in the thirteenth century. After the major legislative changes of 3 February 1295, the number of the members in the Small Council increased to 27. Associated with these men was a priest, parish clerk, a schoolmaster, and an official messenger, all of whom apparently functioned as something like a small bureaucracy to help with official duties. With the exception of the priest, these executives and the members of Small Council were elected yearly at Easter, but only men of the highest levels of society or nobles were known to be chosen for this purpose.[7]

An example of high social status of members in the Small Council was demonstrated on 3 September 1226 when Kuno von Jegistorf held the office of mayor in the community, while his two sons, Peter and Johannes, served in the Small Council. The Small Council was called *consilium* while members of this assembly were referred to as *consules*. Among the many responsibilities of the Small Council was to oversee weights and measures in the city, to control markets, to care for orphans, and to provide police protection. Together, the mayor and Small Council formed the court, which had jurisdiction over the legal affairs of the city. Yet, at times, the mayor could make Judgements by his own authority without the participation of the Small Council. In theory, anyone who had been ejected from the Small Council for some kind of misdeed could not be readmitted, but this appeared to be more a guideline than a practical measure, and it was seldom put into practice.[8]

A document from 1249 stated that there was a 'Council of 50' at that time, but that administrative body later disappeared from the sources. In the major legislative changes of 3 February 1295, the 'Large Council' or 'Council of 200,' and the 'Council of 16' were created, which were also elected yearly at Easter. In the course of the fourteenth century, the office of treasurer was added. The newly acquired lands outside of the town were not included in the city administration and played no direct role in government. In reality, the rulers of the city were also the officials over the entire state. The authority of the city was extended to the lands they controlled by the use of official emissaries who explained and enforced governmental policies, which included judicial authority.[9]

The Council of 16 were important men, who were chosen from the four districts of the city each being represented by four men.[10] These councilmen

6 Karl Geiser, 'Die Verfassung des alten Bern.' *Festschrift zur VII. Säkularfeier der Gründung Berns 1191–1891* (Bern, 1891), pp.112–113.

7 Geiser, 'Die Verfassung des alten Bern,' p.85.

8 Geiser, 'Die Verfassung des alten Bern,' p.104.

9 Geiser, 'Die Verfassung des alten Bern,' pp.85–86.

10 Geiser, 'Die Verfassung des alten Bern,' pp.19–20.

were supposed to look after the interests of the people in their districts. Each member swore to support all functions of the state and their communities in all aspects of government. The Large Council was chosen by the authority of the Council of 16, and the Council of 16 frequently sat with the Small Council, often to counter the influence of the Large Council.[11]

The men in the Large Council were from the lower classes within the city who worked in such occupations as butchers, blacksmiths, bakers, and tanners. These and other craftsmen had begun to organise by the end of the thirteenth century. They formed associations or guilds to protect their economic interests, and they were also politically active by 1293. Guild members were clearly represented in the Large Council in 1295, when a list of 199 names was presented, hence the name Council of 200, and their surnames clearly indicated that these men were from the working classes.[12] The members of this government agency always swore to stand by the state with 'deed and counsel' within or outside the city, which included military assistance whenever necessary. If ever a member of the Large Council failed to follow the direction of the Council of 16, when witnessed by two others, then that man would be punished with a heavy fine and forced to leave the city for one month.[13] Such an expulsion would have been difficult financially for craftsmen, who depended on their crafts and services for employment.

The original intention at the creation of the Large Council was to keep it subordinate to the Small Council and the Council of 16, while giving the assembly of craftsmen the impression that their wishes were being addressed. Yet these men were hardly fooled, and they soon pushed for more influence in the state. In doing so, they had to deal with the impressive power of the noble classes associated with the city, but the workers were often successful and became increasingly important over time.[14] In this sense, Bern was similar to many other cities and towns in the German

Swiss infantry on the march. Diebold Schilling the Younger, *Eidgenössische Chronik des Luzerners*, Lucerne, 1513 (ZHB Luzern Sondersammlung, S 23 fol.)

11 Geiser, 'Die Verfassung des alten Bern,' pp.111–112
12 Geiser, 'Die Verfassung des alten Bern,' pp.19–20.
13 Geiser, 'Die Verfassung des alten Bern,' p.95.
14 Geiser, 'Die Verfassung des alten Bern,' p.95.

Empire and Swiss areas largely in the fourteenth and fifteenth centuries when the guilds competed with noble and aristocratic factions for control of city governments.

Whenever anyone was elected to the Large Council, that man had to attain citizenship, if he had not already done so. The military aspect of a member of the council was affirmed by the end of the fourteenth century because anyone elected to the council by that time must also obtain a war horse and a full suit of armour, including a breastplate, helmet, and metal gauntlets. This armour was so expensive and elaborate that a member of the Large Council in effect had to arm himself similarly to a knight on horseback. This stipulation was simplified later to state that a member of the council need only acquire 'armour and a weapon' to defend the city when called to do so. These men also had to assemble whenever they heard the large or small bells ring at the parish church calling them to arms.[15]

The total population of the city of Bern around the year 1300 was estimated at about 3,000. Of these, less than one quarter would be adult males, and fewer still would lead guilds. This meant that a very large percentage of guild masters would serve sometime on the Large Council. Such a fact was an important aspect of the defence of Bern. While the Small Council was in a position to make its opinions matter the most, the Large Council appeared to have an important influence on the affairs of state. Many of the men in the community felt that the Large Council represented their interests, which included military concerns.[16]

15 Geiser, 'Die Verfassung des alten Bern,' pp.95–96.

16 Hans Delbrück, *Geschichte der Kriegskunst im Rahmen der politischen Geschichte*, vol. 3: *das Mittelalter* (Berlin: Stilke, 1923), p.561.

4

The Battle of Laupen, 21 June 1339

The Function of Banners and Flags

One of the most severe tests of Bern's military abilities and its influence on the nearby areas came with the Battle of Laupen in 1339. Not only was the existence of Bern on the line at that time, but the ability of the tiny Swiss Confederation to extend its power beyond the mountainous areas of its earliest members was put to the test. The cantons of Uri, Schwyz, Unterwalden, and Lucerne would soon have to learn how to manoeuvre in the field and address their adversaries in open battle rather than on mountain slopes. This necessitated a change in organisation and tactics, meaning that flags and banners would play an increasing role in how the Swiss and Bernese deployed and operated in battle. These pennants were so important in the functioning of men in battle that they were often listed as among the most prized articles captured at the end of a successful battle.

The forces at the time of the Battle of Laupen in 1339 always went into battle flying banners and pennants. These items had several functions. They often represented a town, region, occupation, guild, or the kind of weapons wielded by the men. As such, they were a point of pride for the community and among the troops, and the men in the battle formations wanted to stand near their friends, associates, and relatives. In a practical sense, the banners helped men keep the formation of their ranks on campaigns and in battles because they could see the standard and know where they should be stationed. This practice helped keep order in the battle formations and gave the troops a rallying point especially during confusing battles. The most important banner was the state flag which was posted in the centre of the most significant battle formation. As long as this banner still stood, the men knew that the army was in good order. If it fell to the ground or was captured, the men knew their battle formation had been breached, and in all likelihood, they had lost the battle.

Swiss army on the march. Amongst the flags we can see those of Lucerne, Zurich, Bern, Uri and Unterwalden. Diebold Schilling the Younger, *Eidgenössische Chronik des Luzerners*, Lucerne, 1513. (ZHB Luzern Sondersammlung, S 23 fol.)

The various banners, pennants, and flags were held by men known as *Pannerherren*, as well as *Venner* and *Venliträger*. Each of these men had responsibilities related to the carrying one of a number of flags and banners. They could properly be known as the banner men or flag carriers. The *Pannerherren* usually carried city or regional flags, while the *Venner* and *Venliträger* carried banners of less significance, which represented smaller numbers of men. These flag carriers were considered lower officers. Unlike the overall leader of the army, who was often chosen by the head of the government, the men carrying the flags were elected by the troops after the forces had assembled. At that time, all the leaders came together and forgave each other all hate and injury and swore loyalty one to another. The lesser leaders and troops swore to follow the higher officers and the higher officers swore to all the men of the army to lead them as well as possible.[1]

The duty to carry any of the banners or pendants was considered a highly prestigious honour, and only men of high status, best reputation, and known fighting ability would be given this distinction. Of course, the greatest honour was to carry the state or city flag. To prevent a banner's capture often as many as 100 men were assigned to protect it with their lives if necessary. The flags and banners were prized booty for an enemy, and wild and fierce fights often took place around them. In civic militias, the men often assigned to protect the city flag were the blacksmiths who had a reputation of considerable strength, because their occupation often required them to pound the slag out of heated metal by the repeated strikes of a heavy hammer. These men were also used frequently to protect the most vulnerable part of a city's defence, the city gates, again because of their muscular strength.

The men often sought to capture weapons and banners as chief prizes on the field of battle, and the reports of victory in the field almost always included the careful number and listing of captured enemy flags and pennants.[2] When a flag was captured by the enemy, the new one replacing it was marked with a red cross to denote than it, and its army, had been shamed. That sign of remorse was only removed after the flag had been redeemed by enemy blood in battle.[3]

1 Carl von Elgger, *Kriegswesen und Kriegskunst der Schweizerischen Eidgenossen im XIV., XV. und XVI. Jahrhundert* (Lucerne: Militärisches Verlagsbureau, 1873), pp.200–201 and Delbrück, *Geschichte der Krieskunst*, vol. 3, p.620.

2 Frey, *Kriegstaten der Schweizer*, p.475 and Elgger, *Kriegswesen*, p.83 and pp.106–107.

3 Edward A. Gessler, *Das Schweizerische Geschützwesen zur Zeit des Schwabenkriegs*,

Sources on the Laupen War

An understanding of the Laupen War must take into account the nature and relative worth of the primary source materials to assess their importance. The most complete and potentially most reliable source on the war, campaign, and battle at Laupen was the *Conflictus Laupensis* (Laupen War), which was written by an unnamed cleric in Bern. The author lived at the same time as the events he described, thus bringing important contemporary insights into his accounts. Most importantly, he could have spoken with many of the participants in the war, which strengthens any claims to authenticity. As a member of the clergy, the author of the *Conflictus Laupensis* could be expected to bring a religious slant to his narrative, and his history was rich with references to priests and the importance of faith and good works, which aided Bern's victory. The *Conflictus Laupensis* was clearly used by other, later sources, but these other materials often brought additional materials to their accounts.[4]

Swiss infantry defending against the cavalry charges. Bendicht Tschachtlan, Heinrich Dittlinger, *Tschachtlanchronik*, Bern, 1470 (Zentralbibliothek Zürich, Ms A 120)

Conrad Justinger wrote the most detailed description of early Bernese history including the Laupen War, and he presented many details found nowhere else. The weakness of Justinger's work was the fact that he wrote his history in the 1420s roughly 80 years after the events he described. The *Anonyme Stadtchronik* (Anonymous City Chronicle) of Bern follows the *Conflictus Laupensis* closely, and in some areas, it was a translation of the earlier source. The *Stadtchronik* was written in the early fifteenth century, and some of the wording of this source is so similar to that of Conrad Justinger. Yet none of this detracts from the *Stadtchronik*'s importance because it presented additional material that is found nowhere else.[5] The *Cronica de Berno* is another source Justinger used in his history. Even though its account of the Laupen War is quite short, it is still a valuable source with some unique information.[6]

1499 (Zürich: Kommissionsverlag, 1927), p.76; Elgger, *Kriegswesen*, p.122; and Frey, *Kriegstaten der Schweizer*, pp.487–488.

4 *Conflictus Laupensis* in Justinger, *Die Berner-Chronik*, pp.302–313.

5 *Anonyme Stadtchronik* in Justinger, *Die Berner-Chronik*, pp.314–466.

6 *Cronica de Berno* in Justinger, *Die Berner-Chronik*, pp.[295]–301.

Background to the Laupen War

Bern had gained some powerful enemies by its vigorous policy of expansion in the thirteenth century, and various factions had attempted on several occasions to subdue the town in the decades preceding the battle of Laupen. In 1288, the Emperor Rudolf von Habsburg (1218–1291) laid siege to the city twice but failed to overwhelm the municipality, and he was forced to withdraw each time.[7] In the Battle of Dornbühl in 1298, Bern defeated a coalition of nobles in which the Bernese killed an estimated 400 of the enemy and captured another 300. At Dornbühl, Bern fought some of the same antagonists as would be the case at the Battle of Laupen, including the house of Savoy.[8]

The town of Fribourg (Freiburg im Üechtland) was one of the main opponents who would later fight against Bern at Laupen. Fribourg (Freiburg) meant 'free fortress,' which Duke Berchtold IV von Zähringen (ca. 1125–1186) had established in 1157 as a military outpost. To fulfil that role, Berchtold founded it in a defensible position on a sharp bend in the Sarina (Saane) River, so any potential enemy could only approach it with difficulty. The Sarina is a tributary of the Aare River, which flows through Bern. When the dukes of Zähringen died out in 1218, the Kyburg family gained control of Fribourg through inheritance, but the city retained much political autonomy, and it entered alliances with local powers which ironically included Bern in 1243.

The city of Fribourg expanded economically and in size in the thirteenth century, but it entered a graver phase in the political arena when it was sold to the Habsburgs in 1277. This family were the arch-rivals of the independent-minded states and areas nearby, many of whom would later become members of the Swiss Confederation. The Habsburgs were then in competition with the House of Savoy, which was centred in Burgundy at that time, over the control of the region, and Fribourg was repeatedly entangled in the conflicts involving Bern and Savoy. The enmity Savoy held for Bern was understandable because of Bern's 1323 alliance with the Forest Cantons who had inflicted great losses on the nobles at the Battle of Morgarten.[9] The alliance between Fribourg and Savoy included many other noble factions, and the agreement obligated the city on the Sarina to help counter Bern's policy of expansion. This was an important factor in the Battle of Laupen because Fribourg's contribution in manpower in the conflict was significant.

The hostility between Bern and Fribourg entered a more serious phase when King Henry VII of Germany (ca. 1273–1313), later Holy Roman Emperor, ceded the town and fortress of Laupen to Bern in 1310. The cities of Bern and Fribourg are only about 21 miles apart (34.8 kilometres) on

7 Justinger, *Die Berner-Chronik*, pp.31–32.
8 Justinger, *Die Berner-Chronik*, pp.37–38.
9 Justinger, *Die Berner-Chronik*, p.87.

modern roads, and the two urban centres were so close that each could be used as a military staging area for any forces wishing to confront or threaten the other. The fact that Bern owned Laupen gave it additional advantages. Fribourg is about 10 miles (16.3 kilometres) from Laupen, while that fortress is about 16 miles (25.8 kilometres) from Bern. This meant that Laupen was in a strategic location, and the control of that fortress by either side could clearly threaten the other.

Even though Bern's adversaries were numerous and formidable, the city entered into alliance that would make a great deal of difference in the contest to come. Bern and the Forest Cantons started to work more closely together early in the fourteenth century, and the two sides soon began an association that would benefit both parties. The first formal alliance was concluded in 1323. Bern had not yet formally joined the 'eternal pact' of the Swiss Confederation at that early date, and the agreement was relatively limited in scope. But the alliance would mean a great deal in the long run, and this was an important step because Bern was powerful militarily, which would add much to the strength of the Forest Cantons. The most important act of friendship and cooperation came at the Battle of Laupen in 1339 when Uri, Schwyz, and Unterwalden came to Bern's aid at a time of severe crises, and the men of the Forest Cantons contributed significantly to victory in the contest and to the survival of the city.

The struggle, largely between the noble coalition and Fribourg, against Bern in the early part of the fourteenth century was protracted, but the outcome of the Battle of Laupen had much to say about the successful conclusion of the war for Bern. This noble alliance with Fribourg planned to crush Bern from two directions. One army would attack from the west, and it would take the important town and fortress of Laupen and then march directly on Bern. If all went well, another army would march from the east to present a double threat.[10] The plan appeared to be solid, but the large distance between the two armies threatening Bern made the coordination of their efforts most challenging. This allowed the Bernese to react first to the most imminent threat from the west before the other force could deter them from that effort.

Realising the significant threat to Laupen, the Bernese quickly supplied the town and fortress with a large garrison of 600 men. Bern had a policy of splitting family members between the men in fortresses and their relatives in other areas. The idea was that if a man's brother, son, or father was in the garrison, then the troops outside would make every possible effort to come to their aid to avert capitulation, capture, or even execution. Consistent with this policy, the son and namesake of the mayor (*Schultheiss*) of Bern, Johannes von Bubenberg, was sent to the fortress where he commanded the garrison.[11]

10 *Anonyme Stadtchronik* in Justinger, *Die Berner-Chronik,* p.360.

11 *Anonyme Stadtchronik* in Justinger, *Die Berner-Chronik,* p.362.

The Size of Opposing Forces at Laupen

On 10 June 1339, a large army comprised of the factions of nobles and men from Fribourg appeared before the walls of Laupen, and the siege began. The *Conflictus Laupensis*, the most reliable source on the battle, stated that the besieging army consisted of 1,000 cavalry, or helmeted knights, and 16,000 men on foot, which indicated that the force was indeed very large by current standards.[12] Later sources on the battle presented different figures.

The *Anonyme Stadtchronik* stated that the *lantvögte* (overseers or provincial governors) from the Austrian holdings assembled 10,000 men in the Aargau to march on Bern from the east. It was led by Lord Eberhard, Count of Kyburg, burning, plundering, and murdering as he advanced, in an obvious attempt to crush Bern in a vice. These numbers are significant, but the forces were too far away from the scene of action, and they took no direct part in the Battle of Laupen. The numbers presented by other sources were less reliable and appear to be exaggerations. According to the *Anonyme Stadtchronik* and Justinger, the forces in front of Laupen had costly clothing, weapons and mounts, and they numbered 30,000 men on foot. There were also 1,200 *helme* (helmeted) cavalry or knights on horseback. Among them were 700 *krönter helmen* (crowned helmets) from the higher nobility.[13] The author of the *Cronica de Berno* presented similar numbers, and he stated that the men on foot numbered 24,000 men and the helmeted knights numbered 1,200, among whom were 700 crowned knights.[14]

The *Conflictus Laupensis* stated that the number of Bernese troops engaged in the battle was 5,000 with an additional 1,000 men from the Forest Cantons.[15] The *Cronica de Berno* said Bern's forces numbered 6,000, which included 1,200 allies.[16] Justinger asserted that there were 5,000 Bernese which included 900 troops from the Forest Cantons and 450 men from the area of Hasle.[17] The Lords of Weissenburg were the only major group of nobles in the area who supported Bern. Most of the remainder went to war against the Bernese. Also, the majority of the cities and fortresses in the region lined up against Bern with the major exception of Solothurn, which sent 18 'helmets' or well-armed knights to support the Bernese.[18] The small cities of the 'Burgundian Confederacy' of Murten, Payerne, Burgdorf, and Thun were technically allies of Bern as well, but their contribution to the war was minimal at best, and the sources hardly mention them. If these

12 *Conflictus Laupensis* in Justinger, *Die Berner-Chronik,* p.306.

13 *Anonyme Stadtchronik* in Justinger, *Die Berner-Chronik,* p.360 and Justinger, *Die Berner-Chronik,* p.82.

14 *Cronica de Berno* in Justinger *Die Berner-Chronik,* p.300.

15 *Conflictus Laupensis* in Justinger, *Die Berner-Chronik,* pp.306 and 308.

16 *Cronica de Berno* in Justinger *Die Berner-Chronik,* p.300.

17 Justinger, *Die Berner-Chronik,* p.86.

18 Justinger, *Die Berner-Chronik,* p.85.

Austrian army's camp. Bendicht Tschachtlan, Heinrich Dittlinger, *Tschachtlanchronik*, Bern, 1470. (Zentralbibliothek Zürich, Ms A 120)

figures of the opposing forces can be taken at face value, the Bernese were outnumbered from three to one or as much as five to one.

The numbers presented by the primary sources must be taken seriously, but recent studies have given more questionable numbers on the relative size of the two armies. One of the memorials placed at the location of the battle states that each army numbered about 6,000 men, so the forces were roughly equal in size. The eminent military historian, Hans Delbrück, has stated that the Bernese and their allies actually outnumbered their adversaries. 'It may be assumed that Bern with its large territory and the influx [of men] of the Forest Cantons could have placed a larger army in the field than its adversaries, where only Fribourg with a certain general levy [of troops] could appear while the allied lords only assembled with their knights and military auxiliaries in very small numbers.'[19] These assertions that the Bernese were equal or superior in numbers to their adversaries cannot be supported by an examination of the primary source materials, and they are clearly baseless speculations. Incidentally, Delbrück has also been criticised for his anti-Swiss bias in his accounts of their military history.[20]

The numbers presented by the primary sources may be considered the total numbers in the field, but the manpower actually engaged in the battle may have been different. The Bernese may have advanced with much of their total available strength, but there must have been a considerable contingent that remained around Bern itself to counter the threat from the east. That number may have been consequential because the mayor of Bern, Johannes von Bubenberg, senior, remained there to lead the city's defences, while Rudolf von Erlach led the Bernese forces in the field. The

19 Delbrück, *Geschichte der Krieskunst*, vol. 3, pp.589–590.

20 Walter Hadron, 'Neues zur Laupenschlacht,' *Blätter für Bernischen Geschichte, Kunst, und Altertumskunde* 3 (May 1907), pp.120–125.

most notable allies of Bern, the Forest Cantons, only sent three fairly small contingents, and much of their manpower remained at home.

The men from the noble faction needed to lay siege to Laupen may have drained some of their numbers who could have met the Bernese in battle. Likely, these forces were poorly trained to bear arms on the field of battle. Also, the nobles and Fribourg likely came with men designated to care for baggage and equipment used in the siege, and some of them had to operate the siege engines bombarding Laupen. Some men were also needed to protect the camp when the army marched out to attack the enemy, and Peter von Aarberg reportedly led the body of troops who stayed to protect the encampment when the main force marched to meet the Bernese and their allies.[21]

The Quality of Troops facing Bern

Very little is known for certain about the composition and weaponry of the army besieging Laupen. It may be assumed that most of the men on foot were drawn from feudal levies or drafted peasants, who lacked the armour, weaponry, and skill of professional soldiers who were well trained at arms. Presumably, these less competent troops were comprised of men with little or light armour and relatively simple weaponry that consisted mainly of pole arms including spears of various lengths, war scythes, and bills. Such equipment would be consistent with that in use by most footmen of the age. While most of the men supposedly wore typical peasants' clothing, they no doubt recognised that any kind of body armour could be effective in warding off the blows of their adversaries. Chain mail, or any armour made of metal, was expensive due to the cost of manufacture. Yet the men certainly knew the value of a metal helmet in its ability to protect the head from blows struck from above, and such devices could have been highly prized. No doubt, the men would also often wear any kind of padding they could afford for protection, which included leather or layers of cloth on their shoulders, arms, chests and abdomens to deflect or lessen the impact of a blow.

Their weapons would tend to be the least expensive and the most effective for the price. Javelins, or any kind of thrown devices, were rare because they could only be used once, and their effectiveness in battle was questionable. Some crossbows may have been in use, but they were expensive, and only a few men could afford them. If the crossbows were small in number, their impact in battle was limited. Presumably, these men also lacked the necessary weapons training and unit cohesion that would make them capable of advanced manoeuvring, including in the attack and

21 Franz Moser, 'Der Laupenkrieg 1339' in *Archiv des Historischen Vereins des Kantons Bern* 35:1 (1939), p.87.

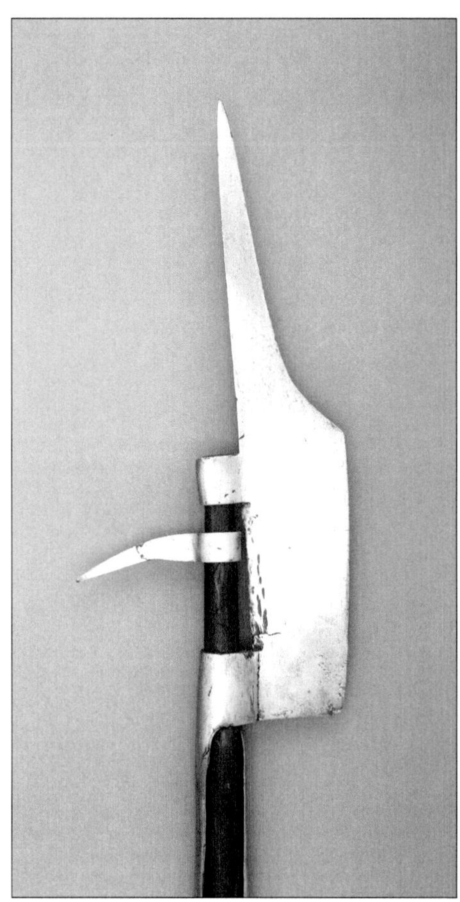

Halberd made in Fribourg in Switzerland, circa 1375–1400. (Metropolitan Museum of Art, New York)

defence, which would make them a match for the more disciplined Swiss. Yet such a large number of men, especially when they heavily outnumbered their adversaries, could be very formidable in simple offensive or defensive roles. One of the distinctions the author of the *Conflictus Laupensis* made between the men on foot (*peditum*) and the cavalry (*equites*) was that the men on horseback were also called helmeted (*galeati*).[22] The knights could be expected to have the good equipment and effective weaponry common to the heavy cavalry of the age.

The author of the *Conflictus Laupensis* stated that the enemies of Bern waged war with severe ferocity. Gerhard von Valengin was a prominent leader of the armies marching against Bern, and he was known for planning the plundering, burning, murdering, and waging a war of extreme violence against the Bernese. Surprisingly, this level of destruction was insufficient, and he wanted to do even worse.[23]

The army arrived before the town and fortress of Laupen the evening before St. Barnabas Day or 10 June 1339. The force came with wagons, horses, and siege engines which probably included catapults and battering rams. The contingents of this army included the entire manpower of Fribourg; the Count of Neuchâtel with many superb knights, whom he had led from Burgundy; the Count of Nidau with his men and 140 helmeted knights from noble lineages, whom he had chosen from Alsace and areas of Swabia in south Germany; the Count of Gruyères; Gerhard von Valengin; Lord Johann the only son of Lord Louis of Savoy; the Lords from the Vaud area; and the Lord of Montenach, each of whom also came with their supporting troops.[24]

The coalition led by a faction of nobles who came to attack Laupen were well prepared for a siege, and they sought to reduce the fortress by the use of catapults. They flung projectiles into the city and fortress day and night. During the siege, over 1,200 stones were counted that had been hurled into the city and fortress. Many if not all of these objects were still useable, and the garrison shot projectiles back at the besiegers inflicting many wounds.[25]

22 *Conflictus Laupensis* in Justinger, *Die Berner-Chronik,* p.306.

23 *Conflictus Laupensis* in Justinger, *Die Berner-Chronik,* p.306. See also, Oechsli, *Quellenbuch*, p.91.

24 *Conflictus Laupensis* in Justinger, *Die Berner-Chronik,* p.306. See also, Oechsli, *Quellenbuch*, p.92.

25 *Anonyme Stadtchronik* in Justinger, *Die Berner-Chronik,* p.363.

These forces laid siege to the town and fortress of Laupen for 12 days all the time showing off all their costly clothing and trappings.[26]

These men besieging the town had an abundance of wine, and they frolicked, showing an abundance of overconfidence. Soon, all the enemies of Bern swore a solemn oath to take the fortress and city of Laupen and to show no mercy and pity to the town and citadel and its inhabitants. They would tear down its walls and hang all its armed inhabitants, inflicting a painful death on them. These adversaries also swore to destroy the city of Bern in a similar manner. Each house would be taken as booty and property, and everything would be held eternally as a matter of right. Afterwards, all the men and women of Bern, including the adults and children, would be completely exterminated or driven out.[27]

Bern's Leadership

Laupen was defended by the detachment sent from Bern, by the local people in the town, and by those of the countryside who fled there for safety. Within the fortress, there was one man who specialised in overseeing the work of the catapults that flung back the stones hurled into the village by the besiegers. This man was Burkhard, the 'master of the machines' (*magister machinarum*). A faction of knights provided the leadership of the Bernese forces of the garrisons of Laupen and Bern. A similar contingent of men with some noble connections led the Bernese army sent to lift the siege at Laupen. Of the ten men mentioned as prominent or with definite leadership positions in the *Conflictus Laupensis*, seven had the preposition *de* (*von* in German) in their name, which usually meant nobility, while three of these were also called lord (*dominus*) as well. In German, these names were Johannes von Bubenberg, senior, Burkhard von Bennenwyle, Burkhard der Werkmeister, Johannes von Seedorf, Berchtoldus Glockner, and Peter von Krantzingen. The flag bearers included Rudolf von Murleren, Peter von Balm, Peter Wentschatz, and Johannes von Herblingen.[28] While leadership of the army was largely in the hands of some men with noble connections which included formal military training, the vast majority of other leaders and the men on foot were clearly from the lowest classes.

Rudolf von Erlach, (ca. 1299–1360) 'a knight' (*ritter*) was clearly a prominent leader of the Bernese army in the field. While the author of the *Conflictus Laupensis* only mentioned Rudolf von Erlach once, and seemingly only in passing, Conrad Justinger stated that he was the overall

26 *Conflictus Laupensis* in Justinger, *Die Berner-Chronik,* p.306 and Oechsli, *Quellenbuch*, p.92.

27 *Conflictus Laupensis* in Justinger, *Die Berner-Chronik,* p.307 and Oechsli, *Quellenbuch*, p.92.

28 *Conflictus Laupensis* in Justinger, *Die Berner-Chronik,* p.307 and Oechsli, *Quellenbuch*, p.92.

Rudolf von Erlach, commander of troops from Bern, praying before the battle of Laupen in 1339. Diebold Schilling the Elder, *Spiezer Chronik*, approx. 1484/1485. (Bern. Burgerbibliothek, Mss.h.h.I.16)

commander of the Bernese and their allies in the battle. Modern scholarship has basically supported the argument that Rudolf von Erlach held that role. Erlach's position of leadership was surprising because the mayor of Bern, Johannes von Bubenberg, senior, would have been expected to hold that responsibility. It appeared that Bubenberg remained in Bern to defend the city in case of attack, while Erlach led the Bernese forces in the field. Clearly, Rudolf von Erlach was held in great esteem, and his command abilities were widely recognised. Yet at the outset of the crisis, his loyalties could be questioned, since Erlach held fiefs from the Lord of Neuchâtel (or Nidau), and was his vassal or 'his servant' (*sin diener*). As such, he was obligated to serve the military interests of the Lord of Nidau who was part of the noble faction fighting against Bern.[29]

War appeared to be unavoidable even before the nobles armed themselves for combat and laid siege to Laupen, and many men had to choose where their loyalties stood. Rudolf von Erlach had strong allegiances to Bern. He was a man whose 'heart' was loyal to that city, 'to his wife and his children, to his friends and associates.'[30] He supposedly spoke directly to the Count of Nidau to explain his loyalties. 'Gracious Lord. It appears to me surely that the war may not be avoided. Therefore, since you and the other nobles want to make war on the people of Bern and accomplish what you will. If I should stay in your good graces, I would have to lose all my possessions that I have in Bern.' The Count of Nidau responded by saying that he could not compensate Erlach for his lost assets, and he must do what he thought best. Erlach responded that as sure as God had granted him life, he must do his best or die.[31] The exchange made the Count of Nidau look understanding, and that Erlach was a man of great morals.

Then Rudolf von Erlach travelled to Bern 'where he was well received, and everyone was pleased with his arrival because he was a proven, pious knight [and] fearless.' He had already demonstrated superb qualities of leadership in six set-piece battles. He would again prove these martial abilities in just a few days. Soon, he was presented before the Small and Large Councils where he was given authority over all the forces of Bern with the understanding that he would have to give battle to raise the siege of Laupen. He should instruct his men on how to conduct themselves with honour and tell them how to start and to end the contest, 'since in war, wisdom is better than strength.' Erlach wanted strict obedience to his

29 Justinger, *Die Berner-Chronik,* p.83.
30 *Anonyme Stadtchronik* in Justinger, *Die Berner-Chronik,* p.361.
31 Justinger, *Die Berner-Chronik,* p.83.

orders, and he only accepted the leadership of Bern under one condition, and that was that the entire community should swear to be obedient to him in all matters. Also, when it became necessary for him to strike or even kill the disobedient in his ranks, he would then not be answerable to all the relatives of those he punished.[32]

Bern's Allies Assemble

The Bernese were in great fear that the town and fortress of Laupen could fall to the besiegers in any given hour. This meant that everyone in the city and castle could be killed or taken prisoner. Within the city were 'many pious men with wives, children, fathers, mothers, brothers, sisters, [and] friends.' All of these were in great danger if the fortress and city were to be captured.[33]

Under such a severe threat, many people of Bern and in Laupen took to prayer and religious services to get the protection of the Lord in their distress. Yet many also turned to more practical measures for defence. Bern made an appeal to all of its allies and friends for help in the crisis and to lift the siege at Laupen, including the Forest Cantons of Schwyz, Uri, and Unterwalden. Even though Bern was a good distance from their lands, these cantons realised that it was in their best interest to support a fight against the power of their arch-rivals, the Habsburgs. In response to the request from Bern, the Forest Cantons stated that since there were so many good people in Laupen who would be killed if the town fell to the enemy, they would support the Bernese in the crisis. They would help protect the people of Bern with their 'body and goods.' Therefore, they immediately ordered that each canton call up 300 well-armed men who were also well supplied. This was a total of 900 men.[34]

Among those answering Bern's call for support was the district of Hasle, which had only been under the authority of the city of Bern for five years. Yet they had sworn to be obedient to the Bernese, and they contributed another 300 well-armed men. Hasle also produced another 150 *Knechte* (squires), who appeared to be troops of an inferior status, for a total of 450 men. Also, the Lord of Weissenburg wanted to satisfy the terms of his citizenship in Bern. He came in person as well as with all his people from a district controlled by him, well supplied and prepared militarily. The people of Bern were happy to see such men of known martial ability join them.[35]

The men of the Forest Cantons were soon involved in a series of forced marches to arrive in Bern as soon as possible, and they advanced day and night. The route these troops took was over the Brünig Pass. The distance

32 Justinger, *Die Berner-Chronik,* p.84.
33 Justinger, *Die Berner-Chronik,* p.84.
34 Justinger, *Die Berner-Chronik,* p.86.
35 Justinger, *Die Berner-Chronik,* p.86.

from Schwyz, the most distant canton to Bern, was about 162 kilometres or approximately 100 miles, and it would take them several days to march so far even when the troops kept up a rapid pace. The men of the Forest Cantons arrived at a location east of Bern after darkness fell on Sunday, 20 June 1339, where they stayed through the remainder of the night.[36]

These men wasted no time, and they marched through Bern early the next morning. When they did so, they found a city in distress. The women and children were lamenting in great sorrow and misery because many of the men had left their homes, and they feared that a large number of them would never return. Through the crying and distress in the city, the people paid little attention to the men of the Forest States, and they made no effort to feed or even to welcome them. The women watched through the night. They cried in the churchyard, and with their devotion to the cross, begged God for his mercy. Also to win favour of the Lord, men and women gave alms to the poor, took vows, and did many other good works.[37]

Early on Monday morning, 21 June 1339, the men of the Forest States marched through Bern to 'brunschüre,' (Brunscheuer) which was located in what is now in the area of Bümpliz, a suburb on the west side of modern Bern, which was on the road to Laupen. The men were well received there and given a meal of 'morning bread.'[38] According to the Julian calendar, 21 June 1339 was a Monday.

Bern's Advance to Relieve the Siege

The Bernese troops also marched out of their city on the morning of Monday 21 June 1339 with all their manpower, flying their city banners, and with all their forces and those of their allies, their 'true friends.' This included Johann von Weissenburg and his men from the lower Simmental area, the 18 prestigious knights from Solothurn, and the men from the Forest Cantons. Many of these troops were well armed, but few had any kind of uniforms, and they wore their usual clothing. Yet each man from the highest to the lowest social order wore a white cross sewn onto his clothing as a means of identification, perhaps as the Forest Cantons did at the Battle of Morgarten. Many of the shields carried by the knights included a white cross on a red background, similar to the state flag of Schwyz.[39] These combined forces marched towards the city and fortress of Laupen to lift the siege and save the people of the town and the beleaguered garrison of 600 men from death or capture.

36 Justinger, *Die Berner-Chronik,* pp.86–87.
37 Justinger, *Die Berner-Chronik,* pp.86–87.
38 Justinger, *Die Berner-Chronik,* p.87.
39 Justinger, *Die Berner-Chronik,* p.87, *Conflictus Laupensis* in Justinger, *Die Berner-Chronik,* p.308, and Oechsli, *Quellenbuch,* p.94.

Pillaging troops. Bendicht Tschachtlan, Heinrich Dittlinger, *Tschachtlanchronik*, Bern, 1470. (Zentralbibliothek Zürich, Ms A 120)

The pace of the march from Bern to Laupen was strenuous, and the rapid advance demonstrated the urgency many felt to raise the siege. The distance from Bern all the way to Laupen on medieval roads was roughly 20 kilometres or about 12½ miles. Yet the armies of Bern and its allies took up a position short of the fortress. Instead, they deployed on a hill roughly two miles or three kilometres from the city, so the actual march was closer to 18 kilometres or 11 miles. These forces arrived at that position before midday (*vor … nachmittage*).[40] Such distance could have been covered in half a day or roughly six to eight hours by men who were used to hard work and long days on farms or herding cattle on steep hills. However, the troops still had the strain of carrying heavy weapons and wearing cumbersome armour for those who had it. They certainly arrived at their position fatigued, and they would soon have to face the physically and mentally demanding ordeal of battle.

The purpose of the campaign was to raise the siege of Laupen, and the best way to accomplish that feat would be to march directly on the enemy forces and launch an attack, but the Bernese and their allies changed tactics as soon as they saw the strength of the enemy. Apparently, the Bernese were poorly informed as to the size of their adversaries. When the Bernese saw the great numbers of their enemy and their many military banners, they abandoned any plan of marching directly on their camp.[41]

Bern's Deployment

The Bernese and their allies then took up a position 'on a small hill' (*ad unum parvulum collem*) now called Bramburg Hill where the battle monument '*Bramburg Denkmal*' now stands.[42] This location was about two miles or three kilometres from Laupen in a straight line, but any approach on that position would have been at a greater distance due to the lay of

40 Justinger, *Die Berner-Chronik,* p.87.
41 Justinger, *Die Berner-Chronik,* p.88.
42 *Conflictus Laupensis* in Justinger, *Die Berner-Chronik,* p.309.

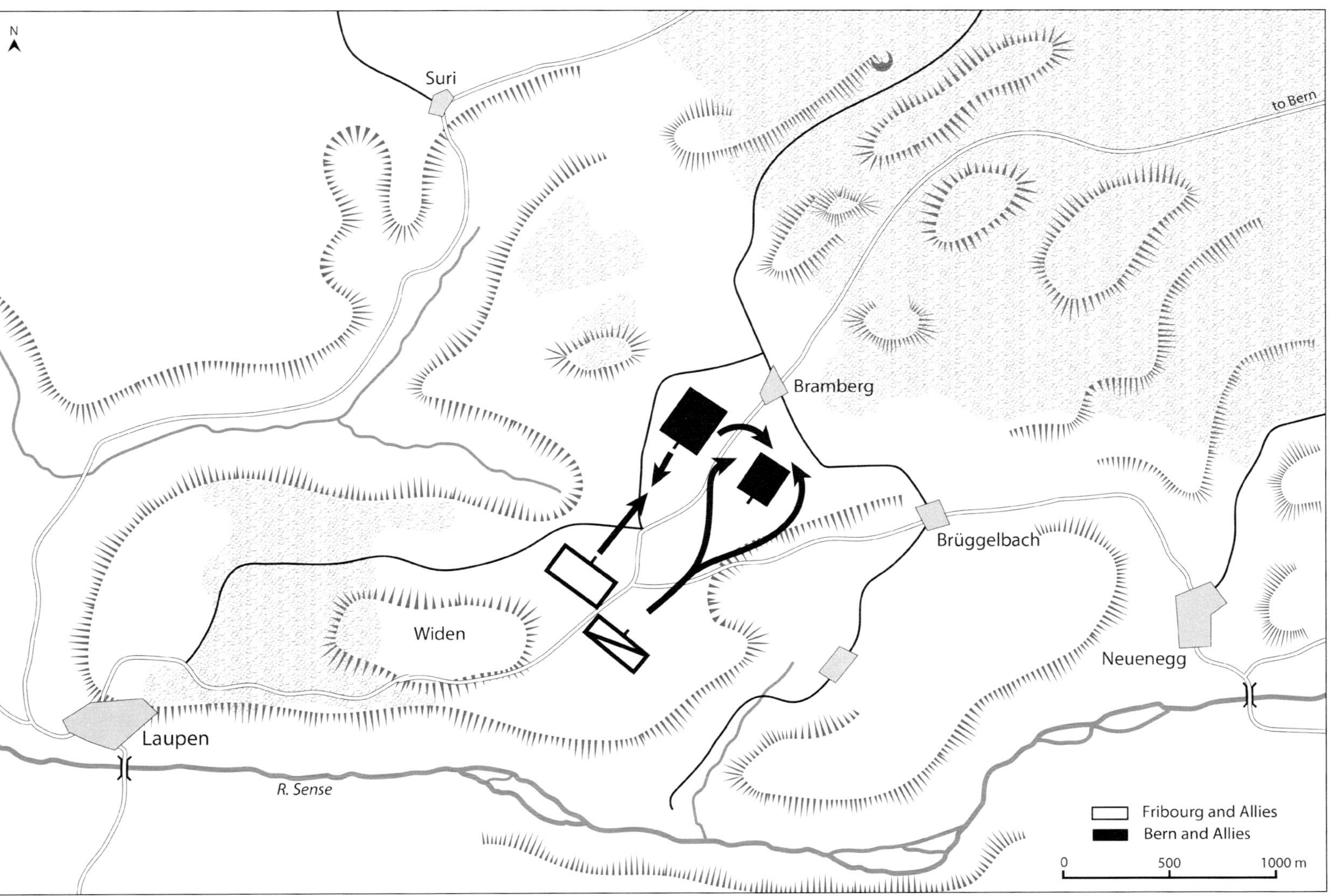

The Battle of Laupen, 21 June 1339

the land and the availability of roads or farm tracks. Bern's halt on the hill meant that there would be little chance of a surprise, and the pause also caused a delay in the action giving Bern's enemies more time to assess the situation, to react, and to prepare a defence or attack. Perhaps the leaders of Bern were hoping that their adversaries would be aggressive and take the battle to the Bernese thus giving them the advantage of fighting on the defensive. If so, they were fortunate, because their enemies soon advanced on their position.

When the Bernese and their allies saw the huge force of the enemy facing them, they all massed together 'just as if in a small wedge' (*quasi unus parvus cuneus*) battle formation.[43] This wedge was clearly an inverted V formation with the point facing the enemy. Such a configuration certainly gave some cohesion to Bern's forces, and the wedge formation had some value when facing enemy foot soldiers. If the best troops from Bern with the appropriate training, weapons, and armour, were placed at the point of the configuration, they could possibly pierce their adversaries' formation of men on foot. This would be most probable if their enemy were poorly disciplined, or if their adversaries' deployment were relatively unstructured.

Yet the wedge disposition had little practical value in facing heavy cavalry. Its sides had to be relatively long, and its centre had to be somewhat narrow, meaning that the formation was comparably vulnerable to a determined charge by the knights who could conceivably cut through it with relative ease. But the disadvantages of the wedge formation were slightly diminished by the fact that the Bernese deployed on the Bramburg Hill, and the course of the battle would demonstrate that the knights were reluctant to attack up the slope to the enemy disposition. A recent examination of the battlefield has shown that the sides of the hill have enough of an incline to cause a cavalry attack to lose some of its impetus as the horses became tired from running up the slope while carrying heavily armoured men.

The forces under Bern were divided into two formations. As mentioned earlier, the Bernese numbered about 5,000 men, and the troops from the Forest Cantons of Uri, Schwyz, and Unterwalden numbered about 900 men. With some men from other groups, this total force was over 1,000 strong. This contingent from the Forest Cantons was clearly highly regarded, and it was placed in a critical position on the battlefield separate from the other formation of men from Bern. As such, the men from the Forest Cantons could protect the Bernese flank, and they were in place also to support the wedge formation as the need might arise.

The position occupied by the men from the Forest Cantons proved to be critical in another sense. The most formidable part of the army facing Bern was the heavy cavalry. These knights were from the noble classes, and they held the men on foot with disdain. Therefore, they wanted to protect their honour and reputation by going into battle in the most prestigious position,

43 *Conflictus Laupensis* in Justinger, *Die Berner-Chronik,* p.309 and Oechsli, *Quellenbuch*, p.94.

and they could be expected to be on the right as the army advanced. Additionally, the distance from the camp of the army besieging Laupen and the Bernese and their allies on the hill was about two miles or three kilometres, and the approach to that position would perhaps take about an hour. That meant that the Bernese and their Confederates had time to view the enemy deployment and arrange their forces accordingly. The best men needed to be positioned to meet the greatest threat, and the men from the Forest Cantons were stationed on the left of the Bernese formation that would soon face the heavy cavalry.

On the other hand, the forces of Bern, Hasle, and the Simmental were stationed to meet the men from Fribourg 'and the other [another] formation (mass) of men on foot' (*und die andren huffen des fusvolkes*).[44] This statement seemed to indicate that Bern's adversaries on foot were in two battle dispositions. While the men of Fribourg were stationed in one of them, the supposition must be that the other formation was comprised of the feudal levies. These forces were given no further mention in the sources, and it may be assumed that they soon joined with the Fribourgers in the battle, or their participation in the contest was largely ineffective.

A Vicious Battle

Since Bern and its allies feared to attack the enemy, which badly outnumbered them, they stood in their positions and saw how the opposing forces left their tents and prepared themselves for battle just as the glow of the fires from the tents climbed up in the sky. The Count of Nidau was the overall commander of the forces besieging Laupen, and when he saw the Bernese forces, he called a battle council among the nobles to decide on the best course of action. Initially, the Count of Nidau was reluctant to engage the Bernese forces, because he saw their numbers and feared heavy casualties, but the nobles said almost in unison that they wanted to engage their enemy. They realised that they had enough time to organise their men and to attack the Bernese before vespers, or before night fell.[45]

The decision to engage Bern and their allies as soon as they were within reach may appear to be a bit rash in retrospect, because the movement ended in defeat. Yet this choice had good logic to support it. The men of Fribourg and the noble factions had time to set their formations, deploy properly, and manoeuvre effectively. The troops of Bern and its coalition had just marched a long distance, presumably in great haste, and could be expected to be tired and perhaps hungry and thirsty as well, while their adversaries had much rest and surely were well fed. The immediate attack

44 Justinger, *Die Berner-Chronik*, pp.88–89.
45 Justinger, *Die Berner-Chronik*, p.88.

might have been a better choice to assure victory for the forces facing Bern rather than a delay.

At the beginning of an important campaign or just before battle, it was common practice for warriors from the noble classes to advance some of their squires or attendants to higher status in the military by dubbing them knights. These squires were young men with at least some noble pretensions, who had reached the required age, shown the appropriate skills, and demonstrated sufficient experience to acquire greater prominence and to take a more crucial role in battle. Apparently, the enemies of Bern had recently bestowed this honour by dubbing these men as knights. These 'new knights' (*novos milites*) were full of bravado, and they jeered at the Bernese by throwing their swords in the air to show their dexterity with that weapon and to intimidate their adversaries with their martial skill. Then, they quickly advanced against the Bernese.[46]

The Battle of Laupen 21 June 1339. Diebold Schilling the Elder, *Spiezer Chronik*, approx. 1484/1485. (Bern. Burgerbibliothek, Mss.h.h.I.16)

About 2,000 Bernese (*duo millia*), who saw the new knights' martial display, became very much alarmed. They then turned and fled into the nearby Forstwald forest for protection and to escape the threat of an able enemy. Among them were a group of men who were unarmed (*inermes*) and had no weapons even though some of them were considered strong and brave in battle.[47] Unarmed men could have had little if any impact on the contest, and they might have even disturbed the armed and more disciplined troops. Perhaps, some of these unarmed men came on the campaign to show their support for the army and to make good their boasts. While each adult male citizen of Bern had an obligation to support the state militarily, when necessary, little is known of any formal military organisation or militia within the city at that time. This fact may account for some unarmed men being with the army.

Rudolf von Erlach's statement may shed light on the matter. 'Then spoke the pious knight Lord Rudolf von Erlach to one of his leaders (*houptman*).' He asked, 'Where are those [men who made] good speeches and their fellows who were so boisterous in the narrow streets of Bern? They should now be standing before the [city] banner. Therefore, come forward.' Those men were recognised as the butchers and tanners at Bern. At least, some of them approached immediately and said: 'Lord we are here and [will] do what you tell us.' Others soon joined them: '[There] were also the other craftsmen, and everyone [was] obedient, no one excepted, and each one did what he should except only those who had fled into the forest.'[48]

46 *Conflictus Laupensis* in Justinger, *Die Berner-Chronik,* p.309.
47 *Conflictus Laupensis* in Justinger, *Die Berner-Chronik,* p.309.
48 Justinger, *Die Berner-Chronik,* p.89.

At least some of the unarmed men found a way to participate in the fight even though their weapons were unconventional. This involved the Swiss tactic of throwing stones at the start of a battle. 'And as they wanted to advance together. Then each took two or three stones as their captain ordered them to do to face the enemy [to throw stones] and then withdraw to stand halfway up the hill.' Some of those who fled seemed to cause others to panic as well. 'Since those in the back thought that those in the front wanted to flee and a great number of men [in the back] fled from the battle formation.' Yet this confusion did not last long, and many found their courage again. 'But when they learned that those in front were still standing in their positions, they returned to the battle and conducted themselves as brave men and fought in the battle and acted as heroes except for a number who fled into the forest and did not return.'[49]

These men who fled and failed to return to the battle were always called 'foresters' in derision. Later, they were punished in 'body and goods,' since their cowardice was believed to have helped the enemy. Apparently, Rudolf von Erlach had something to say about those who fled, and he showed little concern. Some men reported to him, '"O Lord there behind us are fleeing many men from us." Then the leader [Erlach] answered. "It is good that the bad men are not with the brave men. The chaff is separated from the kernel."'[50] However, the rest of the Bernese forces, about 3,000 men, who did not see the flight of the others, stood close together in their battle formation to await the enemy.[51] With the men from the Forest Cantons, the total number would have been about 4,000 troops who soon engaged in battle.

The Lord of Nidau had to be concerned both about the forces facing this army on the hill and the 600 troops in the garrison at Laupen. If Nidau's army removed all the troops besieging Laupen, then the men in the fortress could come out and strike them in the rear. At the very least, the garrison could stage a brief foray from the fortress to burn the camp and destroy or disable the siege engines and devices used to bombard the fortifications. Such a successful raid could have been a major setback for the possible success of the siege, and Nidau needed to deploy enough men to prevent either the attack or the incursion from taking place. The number of troops engaged in the defence of the camp could be modest, but the deployment of forces in the effort would take away some of his manpower from the assault on the Bernese and their allies. Yet Nidau still had his enemies heavily outnumbered. If the estimate of his total force of 16,000 was only a minor exaggeration, and if Nidau left 1,000 to 2,000 men to protect his rear and the siege materials, then the actual number of in his army available to deploy in the attack might have been about 13,000 or 14,000. After the flight of 2,000 men, the Bernese and their allies were about 4,000 men strong.

49 Justinger, *Die Berner-Chronik,* pp.89–90.
50 Justinger, *Die Berner-Chronik,* p.89.
51 *Conflictus Laupensis* in Justinger, *Die Berner-Chronik,* p.309.

A lengthy contest would certainly go against the Bernese because they would eventually be worn down by superior numbers. To be successful in the engagement, the Bernese had to be aggressive and break their enemy's formations early in the battle.

The battle began after vespers, which is just after dusk. This meant that the contest needed to be quickly resolved before nightfall.[52] The knights in Lord Nidau's army focused their efforts on the men of the Forest Cantons, and the heavy cavalry attacked them. The knights soon surrounded the men on foot with their 'terrible' (*terribiliter*) strength.[53] The troops from the Forest Cantons had no choice but to stand on the defence, and they made a formation to withstand any possible cavalry assaults. The nature of this disposition is unknown, but it could have been some kind of circular configuration to allow the men the ability to defend their position from all sides. The contingents from the Forest Cantons had no way of closing with the elusive cavalry and had too few if any crossbows or long pikes that could keep the enemy at bay. The halberd was still an effective weapon, but the attack of a number of heavily armoured knights on horseback could deeply penetrate the Forest Canton's position before the assault could be successfully stopped. While these men on foot were hard pressed, the action was never carried out to its conclusion because the Bernese would soon return to chase the cavalry off the field. Had this fight been allowed to continue, it was uncertain who would have been the final victor. On the other side of the battlefield, the Fribourgers and their allies on foot marched to engage the Bernese infantry.[54]

The decisive moment in the battle took place when Rudolf von Erlach decided to attack the Fribourgers, who were advancing to meet the Bernese. Most of the men in the army of Bern and its allies were wielding the halberd, which was an effective infantry weapon that was used with great effect at the Battle of Morgarten, but it had a major weakness. Even though a skilled soldier could use it effectively in all aspects of battle, it still was a relatively poor weapon when used in the defence. As a two-handed device, it could not be used with a shield or other defensive equipment that required the use of a hand or arm. It could be used to parry the thrust of an enemy's weapon, but it was not designed to do so. It was simply a pole weapon intended to stab or slash, and it was most effective when used in an offensive mode.

Rudolf von Erlach's decision to go on the offensive and order his men to rush their enemies involved a number of risks, including the probable loss of unit cohesion, and the possibility of his men being swallowed up by the larger number of the enemy. The charge also had to be timed perfectly to be successful. If Erlach's advanced was launched too soon, his troops would lose some of their momentum in a downhill charge as they reached more level ground. If he ordered the charge executed too late, much of

52 Justinger, *Die Berner-Chronik,* p.89.

53 *Conflictus Laupensis* in Justinger, *Die Berner-Chronik,* p.309.

54 *Conflictus Laupensis* in Justinger, *Die Berner-Chronik,* p.309.

Infantry clash. Diebold Schilling the Younger, *Eidgenössische Chronik des Luzerners*, Lucerne, 1513 (ZHB Luzern Sondersammlung, S 23 fol.)

the impetus would be lost as his men struck their adversaries. Yet Erlach's onslaught proved to be well-timed. The men from Bern overcame every fear and attacked the ranks of the two formations of the advancing Fribourgers and their allies.[55]

The Bernese threw their stones into their adversaries and then closed with the enemy. The throwing of such projectiles would only be effective if the Bernese attacked in coordination with the hail of stones and then struck at the same time. The adversaries of the Bernese suffered under the heavy blows, and they began to succumb and give way. Part of them were hacked down and fell dead immediately, and some received severe wounds that would later prove to be fatal, while many suffered less severe damage.[56]

At the same time, Rudolf von Erlach was seen near the banner of Bern as he and his men pressed into the enemy and soon cut a hole through their ranks. So many were 'hit and slashed' that they were cut down, and the rest were pushed back. Erlach and his men advanced deep into the enemy formation and forced 'paths and streets' (*wege und strassen*) through enemy so that the man who carried the enemy flag was cut down, and the Bernese captured that banner. Soon, all the rest of the flags were taken, and the enemy banner carriers were killed along with many others. At this point, the Bernese were so victorious that whoever stood before them must either be killed or take a shameful flight.[57]

The most casualties in a medieval battle were typically inflicted when one army broke and ran. At that time, the defeated forces would lose unit cohesion, and the victorious troops could then pursue and cut down their adversaries. The best the fleeing men could hope to accomplish was

55 Justinger, *Die Berner-Chronik*, pp.82 and 90.

56 Justinger, *Die Berner-Chronik*, p.90.

57 Justinger, *Die Berner-Chronik*, p.90 and *Conflictus Laupensis* in Justinger, *Die Berner-Chronik*, p.309.

to escape with their lives. The men from Fribourg and their allies clearly suffered heavy casualties, but they were very fortunate, because many of the victorious Bernese were not in a position to overtake and kill them.

The main reasons why the Bernese did little to pursue their fleeing enemy included the fact that the battle was engaged after vespers, so the darkness of night soon made such an effort more challenging. Most importantly, however, was the fact the fight between the knights and the men of the Forest Cantons was still undecided. The men from the Forest Cantons shouted to the victorious Bernese with a loud voice, 'Dear courageous men of Bern. Turn back to us!' The men of the Forest Cantons were being overwhelmed by the knights, and the Bernese turned to help them in their great duress. The men of Bern struck at the flank of the knights, and the men from the Forest Cantons also attacked in the direction of the advancing Bernese, apparently catching their adversaries in a vice. Once again, the men 'hit and slashed' into the enemy on horseback. The combined efforts of the men from the Forest Cantons and from Bern were so effective that they killed many men in the heavy cavalry. The horses and knights fell to the ground and were killed, while the survivors were put to a shameless flight.[58]

The battle reportedly lasted an hour and a half. The leader of the Bernese, presumably Rudolf von Erlach, called the troops together at the end of the fight to praise God for the victory because the Almighty had stood beside them. The leader also commended his men for being obedient to his orders. The Bernese and their allies were indeed fortunate because they reportedly suffered only 22 dead. Yet the victory was costly in terms of other losses, and the wounded 'of whom there were many' needed to be tended.[59] While the Bernese had directed their efforts to help the men of the Forest Cantons rather than pursue the fleeing enemy, they also abandoned the chase because they wanted to take care of their fellows and allies.[60]

The commander (*houptman*) of the Bernese, no doubt Erlach, and another prominent leader, Johann von Weissenburg, examined the battlefield after the fight. They went from one of the fallen enemy to the others. They recognised all the great Lords and the knights, and Erlach soon ordered their bodies brought to the same place on the battlefield. Many of the dead were from Swabia, Alsace, the Breisgau, the Sundgau of southwest Germany, and the French lands. There soon was a great lamentation in these areas as friends and family members mourned their losses. The mayor of Fribourg laid dead on the battlefield as well as the banner carrier from the same state named Fülisdorf. The losses from Fribourg included the mayor's friends and many more knights, servants, attendants, citizens of all classes, and all sorts of people who accompanied the nobles in the battle.[61] Since the dead included so many men of various social ranks, including those who

58 Justinger, *Die Berner-Chronik,* p.90.
59 Justinger, *Die Berner-Chronik,* p.91.
60 *Conflictus Laupensis* in Justinger, *Die Berner-Chronik,* p.310.
61 Justinger, *Die Berner-Chronik,* p.91.

Infantry clash, Swiss troops on the right. Diebold Schilling the Elder, *Spiezer Chronik*, approx. 1484/1485. (Bern. Burgerbibliothek, Mss.h.h.I.16)

were not deployed as combatants, it may be assumed that these people were in the camp of the besieging army and were killed before they could escape.

The Bernese captured 27 flags, which were important and prestigious military prizes. They also took much valuable property including horses, suits of armour, weapons, clothing, and jewels, which may have been recovered from the nobles' camp facing Laupen. Even second-hand equipment was much in demand, and the amount of material plundered after the battle could have been worth a large sum of money. Peter von Aarberg was with the noble army attacking the Bernese. When he saw that the battle was going against the Fribourgers and nobles, he went back to the encampment where the silver tableware was located. He took it and fled, as a robber and thief, back to Aarberg.[62] At the same time as the Battle of Laupen, the Count of Kyburg, Lord Eberhard, had assembled his men to go into battle against the Bernese, and he approached from the east. His men came to Aarberg on the night of the conflict. When he learned the outcome of the battle, he turned around with his entire force and withdrew.[63]

The Casualties

The men from Bern and their allies remained on the battlefield over night to console many of their wounded and to give them aid. The Bernese also sent word to the people of Fribourg that whoever wanted to come and retrieve the bodies of the dead could do so without any fear of interference. Afterwards, the nobles and many other important people from Fribourg and other areas came, and they dug graves on the battlefield to bury their dead in large pits. According to Justinger, about 4,500 of the enemies of Bern had been killed. Yet, by the time Justinger wrote his account of the battle in the 1420s, the numbers of men killed in the contest had become controversial. As he explained, 'Some say more. Some say less. I have chosen a number in the middle. God well knows the right number.' Justinger never explained who were saying 'more' or 'less.'[64] Other sources differ on the number of casualties that Bern's enemies suffered in the battle. The author of the *Anonyme Stadtchronik* stated that 4,000 dead lay on the battlefield.

62 Justinger, *Die Berner-Chronik*, p.92.
63 Justinger, *Die Berner-Chronik*, p.92.
64 Justinger, *Die Berner-Chronik*, pp.92–93.

While 'some of the other chroniclers (*andren kroniken*) say there were many more [dead].'[65] Who these 'other Chroniclers' were remained unknown.

The more reliable *Conflictus Laupensis* presents a lower number of fatalities, and the author said 1,500 enemies of Bern lay dead on the battlefield.[66] The *Oberrheinische Chronik* also stated that the number of the fallen was 1,500.[67] This figure is reasonable, but other numbers have been presented, which tend to complicate the issue further. Johannes von Winterthur stated that the loss was nearly 1,000 on each side of the contest.[68] The Dominican monk, Heinrich von Nördlingen, wrote directly after the battle to Sister Margaretha Ebner, a nun in Maria-Medingen Convent. He stated that on the last Monday before John the Baptist Day, 21 June 1339, Bern and Schwyz had killed 1,600 men, and among them were six counts and many knights, the best of the land.[69] Viewing the number of losses for the enemies of Bern conservatively, the most reasonable estimate might be from 1,000 to 1,500.

There is yet another disturbing factor which must be considered when discussing fatalities. Research going back centuries clearly indicated that relatively few men are killed outright in a battle, and a greater number of men suffer from wounds. This was almost always the case even with the use of the enormous destructive capability of modern, mechanised warfare. If properly cared for, wounded men, even in the Middle Ages, had a reasonable chance of recovery. If not, many would certainly die. The sources on the Battle of Laupen give very little information on how or if the wounded of the enemies of Bern were retrieved, consoled, or treated. Maybe such aid was simply outside the interest for the writers to record. This possibility is a bit surprising since the *Conflictus Laupensis* was written by a churchman, and he would be expected to record any compassion that was shown to the wounded. The author of the *Conflictus Laupensis* and Conrad Justinger went to great pains to show that the Bernese and their allies were pious, meaning the victory came as a gift from God. This leaves the disturbing likelihood that the enemy wounded were either left to die on the field of battle, or that they were killed to put them out of their misery.

Since the Bernese and their allies were victorious, their number of dead would be expected to be far less than their defeated enemies. As already mentioned, Justinger placed the number of dead at 22. Two centuries after the battle the famous Swiss historian, Aegidius Tschudi, gave some additional information on the numbers of the dead. He stated that there were 22 who died from Bern and 13 from the Forest Cantons.[70] Many Swiss areas had

65 *Anonyme Stadtchronik* in Justinger, *Die Berner-Chronik,* p.368.

66 *Conflictus Laupensis* in Justinger, *Die Berner-Chronik*, p.309.

67 *Oberrheinische Chronik*: Älteste bis jetzt bekannte in Deutscher Prosa, Karl Grieshaber, (ed.) (Rastatt, 1850), p.34.

68 Johannes von Winterthur, *Chronik*, p.148.

69 Moser, 'Der Laupenkrieg 1339,' p.93.

70 Moser, 'Der Laupenkrieg 1339,' p.93.

Cavalry charge. Diebold Schilling the Elder, *Spiezer Chronik*, approx. 1484/1485. (Bern. Burgerbibliothek, Mss.h.h.l.16)

a book of yearly commemoration of the dead (*Jahrzeitbuch*) who died in battle, which prove to be valuable sources on many conflicts throughout the Middle Ages. In the small region of Schachdorf in the Schachen Valley (Schächenthal) of the Uri Canton, the book of commemoration listed the names of the four men known to have died in the Battle of Laupen. They were Heini zu dem Brunnen, Konrad an der Gand, Welti Kunders Sohn am Hoffacher, and Walter Weffler.[71]

Surprisingly, the fatalities of those who fought with Fribourg included many important nobles. Normally, the men on horseback could flee the battle when their position was gravely threatened to get out of harm's way and to save their lives. The high casualty figures the knights suffered might mean that they were trapped or crushed between the two forces when the Bernese came to rescue the troops from the Forest Cantons. Frequently in battle, nobles were captured whenever possible, because they could be held for ransom often at a very high price. Yet the sources say almost nothing about prisoners held after the battle meaning there was either no opportunity to take them, or that they were killed rather than captured.

Among the illustrious dead of the noble faction that faced Bern were Lord Johann, the son of the Lord Ludwig of Savoy; the Lords of the Vaud; Lord Rudolf, Count of Nidau; the Lord Gerhard von Valengin; Lord Johannes von Maggenburg; the knight and mayor from Fribourg, and various other knights and nobles. Numerous others were killed whose names were not recorded. The Bernese captured 27 flags and 80 'crowned helmets' from the more important nobles as well as the booty plundered from the dead.[72]

71 'Die Berner entsetzen die burg Laupen,' in *Fontes Rerum Bernensium: Bern's Geschichtsquellen* 10 vols. 6 (Bern: K. Schmidt, 1887–1956), p.483 and Moser, 'Der Laupenkrieg 1339,' p.94.

72 *Conflictus Laupensis* in Justinger, *Die Berner-Chronik,* pp.309–310 and Oechsli, *Quellenbuch*, p.95.

Celebration and Friendship after the Battle

The men in the garrison of Laupen, and the people in the fortress, initially had little knowledge of how the battle was proceeding, because they could only see a limited distance and were unsure about the outcome of the contest. They cautiously failed to sally out of the town to attack the enemy rear, and they also neglected to rush out of the fortress in an attempt to destroy their adversaries' siege machinery or to burn the enemy camp. Only after the Bernese had killed the enemy or put them to flight were they able to get the message of victory to the garrison at Laupen.[73] The men in the victorious army and the people inside the fortress soon staged a great celebration. This was especially the case because both groups knew that the Bernese had been outnumbered heavily and had been victorious despite the odds. Yet the men in the Bernese army stated that if the garrison of 600 men in Laupen had joined the fight, they would have helped a great deal in the battle.[74]

The day after that battle was a Tuesday, 22 June 1339, which was the celebration of the day of 10,000 Martyrs, and many saw a religious significance in the victory. There was great joy and much gaiety because of the victory, and many people performed religious rituals to give thanks including presenting offerings to the church and giving alms to the poor. The people of Bern stated that they and their descendants would always remember the victory, and they would stage religious processions yearly with the holy cross as a day of commemoration.[75]

When the troops from the Forest Cantons marched back to Bern, the people of that city greeted them and gave them great thanks with a large

Swiss army on the march. Well visible are flags of different cantons. Diebold Schilling the Younger, *Eidgenössische Chronik des Luzerners*, Lucerne, 1513. (ZHB Luzern Sondersammlung, S 23 fol.)

73 *Conflictus Laupensis* in Justinger, *Die Berner-Chronik*, p.310.
74 Justinger, *Die Berner-Chronik*, p.92.
75 Justinger, *Die Berner-Chronik*, p.93 and *Conflictus Laupensis* in Justinger, *Die Berner-Chronik*, p.310.

celebration. The citizens of Bern assured the men of the Forest Cantons that their great service and friendship would never be forgotten. They also stated that this gratitude would be passed to their descendants. The Bernese also assured the men of the Forest Cantons that they would help them with 'body and goods' whenever called to do so. The men from the Forest Cantons left Bern feeling great friendship and returned home cheerfully. Also, the men from Weissenburg, those from the Simmental, and the 18 helmets from Solothurn were given great thanks, and they returned home joyfully and in good spirits as well.[76]

The War Continues

The victory at the Battle of Laupen was highly significant in the history of warfare and in the future viability of the Swiss Confederation, but it failed to decide the war, so it was not entirely conclusive. In fact, the victory was only the beginning of a long feud to be fought between Bern and their followers against Fribourg. Yet after the battle, the nobles and their allies were reluctant to engage Bern in the open field of combat, and they soon changed tactics.[77]

The losses suffered by the enemies of Bern included many of the leaders of the noble factions, and their forces stood more in the background on further operations. Many of the losses were replaced when the Habsburgs became more involved later in the war.[78] Also, the casualties Fribourg suffered were insufficient to cripple its ability to continue the conflict. In fact, Fribourg was literally thirsting for revenge for its shame and disgrace, and the city ravaged Bern's lands until the weeks after the next Easter, which fell on 16 April 1340 that year. Therefore, the war would continue in intensity for over another ten months after the battle.[79] For their part, the Bernese also wanted to prosecute the war to a successful conclusion, and they reportedly vowed, 'We no longer want to lay like a cripple in bed! Take heart! We want to stir ourselves [to action] and bring the war to an end.'[80]

The Fribourgers waged a war of exhaustion, strangulation, and starvation by burning and plundering in a policy of constant warfare. In their viciousness, they killed without mercy all the people they surprised in their attacks. In this effort, the illustrious Habsburgs and their supporters sent aid to the Fribourgers by dispatching troops, comfort, and money to them, so the city could continue the fight against Bern on a daily basis. The warfare was so consistent that the Bernese deployed men in the field day

76 Justinger, *Die Berner-Chronik,* pp.93–94.
77 Dändliker, *Geschichte der Schweiz*, vol. 1, p.506.
78 Dändliker, *Geschichte der Schweiz*, vol. 1, p.506.
79 *Conflictus Laupensis* in Justinger, *Die Berner-Chronik,* p.310.
80 Dändliker, *Geschichte der Schweiz*, vol. 1, p.506.

and night to meet the constant threat.[81] The Habsburgs and Fribourgers were so successful in their war of attrition that they forced the cities of Solothurn, Biel, Murten, Payerne, and Thun to abandon Bern, and these former allies sent neither food nor military aid to their former associate. Bern was almost in a state of siege, and it was opposed nearly on all sides, so the city was unable to import supplies or foodstuffs, specifically wine and dairy products. At times, Bern had to bring in goods with an escort in a similar manner to a military expedition. This was the case when the Bernese marched out in military formation with city banners flying to bring in supplies from the town and fortress of Spiez. Luckily for the Bernese, they also received food from Unterwalden and Hasle about the same time. Bern was pressed and plagued by these problems until after Easter of 1340.[82]

The leaders of Bern realised it would be best to take the fight to the enemy, and they finally felt strong enough to go on the offensive against Fribourg and its allies. One of the early attempts to advance on Fribourg by a strong contingent of Bernese troops ended in defeat. About 40 knights and their retainers advanced on that city, but the Fribourgers were warned of the Bernese approach, and they marched out to meet them with a large force. In this case, 22 men from Bern were killed and the remaining 18 came sorrowfully back to the city.[83] In the week between Palm Sunday and Easter which was about 10 to 16 April 1340, the forces of Bern marched to the city of Huttwil. The Count of Kyburg owned the fortress, and it was well protected with formidable walls and effective entrenchments. Johannes von Bubenberg, the elder, who was also the mayor of Bern, led a force of knights and men on foot with the city banner. The heavy cavalry advanced first on Huttwil, took the city, and had set it on fire before the men on foot reached their destination. The men from Bern plundered Huttwil and burned it to the ground. Those defending the city were killed, and the remaining citizens were led away into captivity.[84]

On the Tuesday following the Easter week, 25 April 1340, the Bernese marched out under the command of Rudolf von Erlach without the aid of their allies. Flying all the city banners and wielding their weapons, they advanced to the city of Fribourg roughly 35 kilometres or about 22 miles away. This was a significant distance to be covered on foot from sunrise to sunset, but it was within reach of men who were used to walking long distances on foot as part of their vigorous lifestyle as farmers and herders. While they could have reached their destination on the same day, they also might have arrived a day later.[85]

81 Justinger, *Die Berner-Chronik,* p.96.

82 *Conflictus Laupensis* in Justinger, *Die Berner-Chronik,* pp.310–311 and Justinger, *Die Berner-Chronik,* p.97.

83 *Conflictus Laupensis* in Justinger, *Die Berner-Chronik,* p.311 and Justinger, *Die Berner-Chronik,* p.97.

84 Justinger, *Die Berner-Chronik,* p.97.

85 *Conflictus Laupensis* in Justinger, *Die Berner-Chronik,* p.311.

Swiss infantry. Diebold Schilling the Younger, *Eidgenössische Chronik des Luzerners*, Lucerne, 1513 (ZHB Luzern Sondersammlung, S 23 fol.)

The Fribourgers foolishly left their city's defences and marched out to face their enemies at Schönberg just outside the town. They apparently had little idea of the size of the forces facing them, and they turned away and retreated from the Bernese once they saw the approaching army. The forces of Bern pursued the fleeing Fribourgers all the way to the city gates. In the ensuing confusion, 700 Fribourgers drowned in the Sarine River. The author of the *Conflictus Laupensis* said that Rudolf von Erlach fought just like a powerful lion, who knows no fear. He would never pull back in terror from any beast and would never be horrified. On the same day, the Bernese forces stormed, plundered, and burned the fortress of Castel which was controlled by Fribourg.[86]

The men from Bern also marched to the fortress of the knight, Jordan von Burgistein, a vassal of the Austrians and an ally of Fribourg. He was known to have taken a major role in formenting the war. Jordan Von Burgistein had stood in the ranks with the nobles facing Bern at the Battle of Laupen, and when the 2,000 Bernese fled in fear to the forest, he was quite happy, and the knight observed. 'This is a good blacksmith who has forged this war and everything against Bern.' The year after the battle the Bernese laid siege to his castle, and Burgistein apparently looked outside the window of his fortress to get a better view of the situation. He neglected to put on his helmet at that time, and he was shot and killed by a bolt from a crossbow fired by a 'good fellow' from Bern named Vifli or Vischli. The Bernese then commented, 'That was a good blacksmith who forged that bolt.' Soon after, the Bernese stormed the castle, and they then tore it down.[87]

On the next Thursday (*feria quinta*) or 27 April 1340, the Bernese again marched on Fribourg where they plundered what apparently was a suburb of the city called Galteren. They then set all the houses on fire leading to the bridge going into the city. The Fribourgers were in such fear at the sight of the Bernese that many of them took their possessions to the other side of the city and appeared to flee through the city gate.[88] The fortunes of the Bernese were so high everywhere at that point that many people said, 'God obviously fights for the Bernese and their rights, and it appears that God is a citizen of Bern.' The chronicler, Conrad Justinger, had a slightly different take on these opinions. He wrote that many people observed, 'God has

86 *Conflictus Laupensis* in Justinger, *Die Berner-Chronik,* p.311.

87 Justinger, *Die Berner-Chronik,* pp.95–96 and *Anonyme Stadtchronik* in Justinger, *Die Berner-Chronik,* pp.374–375.

88 *Conflictus Laupensis* in Justinger, *Die Berner-Chronik,* p.311.

become a citizen of Bern, [and] who wants to fight against God?'[89] Finally, Bern's enemies and adversaries were fatigued and broken by their many misfortunes. Moreover, the Bernese were also exhausted by their many struggles and ordeals. Both sides wanted to return to peace and harmony, but these adversaries had to find an intermediary to negotiate a settlement of the conflict.[90]

Agnes of Hungary Negotiates the Peace

The mediator for peace negotiations came from an unlikely source, Agnes of Austria, also known as Agnes von Ungarn (Agnes of Hungary). Agnes was born about 1281 and died in Königsfelden near Windisch in 1364, which is in the modern Aargau Canton of Switzerland. She was a Habsburg princess and was the daughter of the Holy Roman Emperor, Albert I (Albrecht I), who was famously murdered in 1308. She married the Hungarian King Andrew III (Andreas III) in 1296 when she was roughly 15 years old. The couple had no children, and when her husband died in 1301, Agnes returned to the Habsburg areas. She took the vows of a nun and stayed much of the rest of her life in a convent in Königsfelden. The cloister was near the ancestral castle of the House of Habsburg, the *Habichtsburg* or Hawk's Castle.[91]

Swiss infantry, well visible different types of polearms being used. Bendicht Tschachtlan, Heinrich Dittlinger, *Tschachtlanchronik*, Bern, 1470. (Zentralbibliothek Zürich, Ms A 120)

As a Habsburg, Agnes would have been expected to support the position of her family, but she had earned a reputation of being impartial in negotiations, so both sides of any dispute tended to trust her. She functioned as an intermediary in many conflicts, and she had already achieved an important diplomatic success in brokering a peace between Bern and Fribourg at the end of the Gümmenenkrieg from 1331 to 1333. Finally, both sides of the Laupen War had become exhausted, and they sent out peace feelers. Bern came eagerly to the negotiations to be relieved from the extensive privations of the war. Its emissaries came to Königsfelden in the late summer of 1340 to consult with Agnes, who was considered to be no ordinary woman, being described as 'manly and strong.' Agnes negotiated an armistice in which both sides agreed to refrain from any military action from 10 August until 29 September 1340.[92]

89 Justinger, *Die Berner-Chronik*, p.102.

90 *Conflictus Laupensis* in Justinger, *Die Berner-Chronik*, p.313.

91 Hermann von Liebenau, *Lebens-Geschichte der Königin Agnes von Ungarn: der letzten Habsburgerin des erlauchten Stammhauses as dem Aargaue* (Regensburg: Mainz, 1868)

92 Justinger, *Die Berner-Chronik*, p.102 and Dändliker, *Geschichte der Schweiz*, vol. 1, p.507.

First, Agnes arranged a peace between her brothers and uncles, the dukes of Austria, and the city of Bern.[93] The two principal antagonists, Bern and Fribourg, managed to reach a formal peace agreement late in the same year. Agnes maintained that the circumstances at the beginning of the war should be reinstated, and every imposition made against Bern should be withdrawn. Bern was reconciled and renewed all old alliances with the cities in the area, including Fribourg. No formal treaty was made with the German Emperor, so a state of hostility was retained with him at least for the time being.[94]

Laupen Strengthens the Swiss Confederation

The loyalty and the strength of the Forest Cantons impressed Bern, so that city renewed its old alliance with them in the summer of 1341. This agreement obligated both parties to come to each other's aid in the case of a war with the German Emperor within the next ten years. For the remainder of the Middle Ages, the memories of Laupen, Erlach, and the Day of 10,000 Martyrs would awake great feelings of courage and patriotism among the Swiss. Nearly a century and a half later, during the Burgundian Wars (1474–1477) when the Swiss fought the last major threat from a noble coalition, the memory of courage, enthusiasm, and fortitude from the Battle of Laupen still inspired the members of the Confederation.[95]

There were many long-term effects of the Battle of Laupen, which fostered an attitude of cooperation and mutual support between Bern and the Forest Cantons. In 1425, Schwyz marched over the Alps with 500 men using the St. Gotthard Pass to regain some of the losses they had suffered after the Battle of Arbedo in 1422. The troops took the castle of Thum, but they were soon besieged by an army from Milan. The Schwyzers were in a desperate situation, and they sought Bern's aid. Schwyz sent two old men to Bern to plead for help from that city council. The appeal was to the friendship the two states had long shared. The city government made the decision rapidly. The council replied that they had good feelings toward Schwyz, since that canton had helped the Bernese at the Battle of Laupen. The army was called out, and in three days 5,000 men were marching to raise the siege. The situation was resolved before heavy combat took place, but the Bernese were certainly willing to aid Schwyz in the affair because they remembered the support they received at the Battle of Laupen.[96]

---

93 'Die Königin Agnes von Ungarn vermittelt einen Frieden zwischen ihren Brüdern und Oheimen, Den Herzogen von Oesterreich, und der Stadt Bern,' 9 August 1340 *Fontes Rerum Bernensium*, 6, pp.536–540.

94 Justinger, *Die Berner-Chronik,* p.105 and Dändliker, *Geschichte der Schweiz*, vol. 1, p.507.

95 Dändliker, *Geschichte der Schweiz*, vol. 1, pp.507–508.

96 Justinger, *Die Berner-Chronik,* pp.280–283.

Even though the association was strong, Bern was not yet a full member of the Swiss Confederation.[97] The pressures and threats from the Habsburgs and other hostile areas helped Bern realise that a closer and permanent association with the Confederation was in its best interest, so the Bernese formally joined the 'eternal' alliance in 1353.[98]

Not only did the victory at Laupen help convince Bern to join the Swiss Confederation, but other cantons nearby also realised that joining the alliance was in their best interest, and new members became part of the Three States' Pact about the same time. As already mentioned, Lucerne joined in 1332. Zurich became a member in 1351, which meant that another important city economically and militarily would strengthen the alliance. Both Zug and Glarus joined in the agreement in 1352. None of the texts of the documents showing new members had joined refers to the Federal Charter of 1291, but each treaty is a milestone in the development of the Swiss nation.[99] Together, these states formed the 'Eight Old Areas [Cantons]' (*Acht Alte Orte*), which were the political union that helped the Swiss Confederation to survive and acquire new members in the fifteenth century. The union of these cantons also meant that the coalition would be even more important militarily in the coming decades.

Not only was the Battle of Laupen highly significant for the preservation of Bern and the strength of the Swiss Confederation, but it had an important impact on the history of warfare. Despite the fact that infantry tactics and weaponry required additional advancements to meet the challenges of warfare during the late Middle Ages, an advancement in effectiveness of men on foot had been demonstrated. For one of the first times in the era, an organised peasant army was able to defeat a competent force of heavy cavalry in a contest on open ground that would normally favour the knights. There would be many other such victories to come that advanced the history of warfare, including more successes by the Swiss and their allies.

The Bernese had attempted to marshal a huge portion of the population of the city for the campaign against the forces besieging Laupen, which led to the use of men who were unprepared in either training or weaponry to face battle. The concept of an army from the masses was clearly in its infancy as far as Bern was concerned, and a truly effective force recruited from the civic population did not yet exist. A sophisticated infantry formation, the wedge, was used in the battle, showing that there was a good knowledge at hand on infantry tactics. However, future developments were necessary because a wedge was not as effective against heavy cavalry as against infantry. Its sides were too long, thus allowing for many places of possible penetration, and

97 Dändliker, *Geschichte der Schweiz*, vol. 1, p.507.

98 Dändliker, *Geschichte der Schweiz*, vol. 1, pp.529–549.

99 Oechsli, *Quellenbuch*, 'Der Luzerner Bund. Luzern, 7. Nov. 1332,' pp.81–83; 'Der Zürcher Bund. Zürich, 1. Mai 1351,' pp.97–102; 'Aus dem Glarner Bund, 4. Juni 1352,' pp.104–106; 'Der Zuger Bund. Luzern, 27. Juni 1352,' p.106; and 'Der Berner Bund. Luzern, 6 März 1353,' pp.107–110.

its depth was insufficient to withstand heavy cavalry attacks. It would be more than a century before the development of weaponry and tactics was sufficient to meet all the challenges of the warfare of the age.

Erlach's Murder: Death of a Hero

After the Laupen War, Rudolf von Erlach never led another major military operation, and he was little involved in politics as well. He largely appeared in the sources only as an arbitrator or as a witness in legal cases. He bought property in Reichenbach north of Bern where he lived in a castle in the later years of his life. He is believed to have met a sad end there. Erlach got into a dispute with his son-in-law, Jost von Rudenz from Unterwalden, over the amount of the money owed him as part of his wife's dowry. In 1360, Rudenz came to the Castle of Reichenbach in a rage and confronted the aged military leader in one of the rooms of the fortress. Outside the room in a corridor, hung the sword Erlach had wielded in many military operations including the Battle of Laupen. Rudenz grabbed the weapon, went into the room and stabbed the hero of Laupen to death. The murderer fled from the castle, and he was nearly overtaken and killed by Erlach's two dogs who heard the commotion and came after him. When news of the deed reached Bern, a large number of people came looking for him with the intention of breaking him on the wheel as a common murderer. Rudenz had to make good his escape, or he would have suffered a very painful death.[100] Rudolf von Erlach's memory is still preserved in Bern, and he is honoured by a statue in the Erlach memorial in the Ringgepark near the centre of the city.

Rudolf von Erlach murdered by his son-in-law, Jost von Rudenz, in 1360. Diebold Schilling the Elder, *Spiezer Chronik*, approx. 1484/1485. (Bern. Burgerbibliothek, Mss.h.h.I.16)

100 Justinger, *Die Berner-Chronik*, p.124 and Dändliker, *Geschichte der Schweiz*, vol. 1, pp.508–509.

5

The Swiss meet the English: The Gugler Invasion

Among the most respected and successful foot soldiers in the later Middle Ages were the English yeomen and the Swiss, but the two infantries employed significantly different weapons and tactics. Since the English wielded the very powerful longbow, which has been called the 'medieval machine gun,' there can be little doubt what would have happened if the two armies had met on a broad field of battle where the weapon could be used effectively. Yet English mercenaries and Swiss peasants were involved in a number of clashes in the Gugler invasion of 1375 with surprising results.

The English were deeply involved in the properly-named Hundred Years' War (1337–1453). While the main contest was between the kingdoms of England and France, the conflict was so long and so broad in scope that other states became involved, and military actions that took place in many outlying areas including the Swiss cantons. The major confrontation between the Swiss and the famous English yeomen during the era of the Hundred Years' War took place in 1375. The clash did not result in a major battle, so a test of strength in a large engagement never occurred. But the small actions that resulted from the English invasion did demonstrate some of the Swiss military abilities.

There was a near confrontation between the English and Swiss in 1365 when the English invaded Alsace near the Swiss lands. This included the city of Basel. This city on the Rhine River had suffered a devastating earthquake in 1356, which was clearly recognised as the most severe earthquake ever to hit in the middle of Europe. The shock was so severe that the city walls were damaged and huge sections of the town burned as well. Basel was already reeling from the loss of roughly half of its population in the Black Death of 1348, and the community had been unable to reconstruct some of the defensive fortifications in the years following the earthquake.[1]

1 Ludwig Sieber, 'Zwei neue Berichte über das Erdbeben von 1356,' *Beiträge zur*

One of Basel's suburbs was dangerously exposed to the possibility of attack, and the city sent an appeal to various cantons including Bern, Lucerne, and Zurich for military aid. According to Justinger, a contingent of 1,500 men from Bern soon arrived. Another Swiss chronicler, Petermann Etterlin, stated that these troops came from Bern, Zurich, and other lands. Despite the fact that the forces of the English and Swiss were near each other, no confrontation took place at that time, because the danger soon passed when the yeomen failed to advance on Basel.[2] The cooperation between Basel and Bern in 1365 was remarkable because there would soon be a turn of events, and Bern was then at war with the Bishop of Basel, Johann von Vienne, from 1367 to 1368. The war was costly, and the Bishop even burned the city of Biel, when it switched alliances from Basel to Bern. Yet the war finally ended and relations between Basel and Bern again became friendly.[3]

On occasion, the Hundred Years' War enjoyed brief truces when fighting was supposed to stop, but military operations frequently continued at these times even though such actions had no official approval. This was the case when the English invaded Swiss lands in 1375. A one-year truce was signed between Charles V of France and Edward III of England in June of 1375. This agreement immediately threw large numbers of English and French mercenaries out of work, and they no longer received provisions or pay from their former employers. To survive, these men were forced to pillage the local people for their necessities. The troops also sought to take as much plunder as possible and seized anything of value. The problem of these unregulated forces ravaging the countryside was partially solved by sending some of them to foreign lands on what the historian, Barbara Tuchman, has called the 'great riddance.'[4]

The leader of these soldiers was Enguerrand VII de Coucy (1340–1397). Even though he was a Frenchman, Coucy had strong connections to England. Despite the fact that his family owned extensive lands in northeastern France in the Picardy region, they also inherited areas in England from Coucy's great-grandmother, Catherine de Baliol, which included holdings in Yorkshire, Lancashire, Westmoreland, and Cumberland. After the English captured King John II of France at the famous Battle of Poitiers in 1356, negotiations for his release lasted years. Coucy was sent to England with 40 hostages as a statement of good faith as the diplomatic discussions continued. He remained there for five years. He first met King Edward III in 1359, and that monarch took a liking to the elegant young man. In fact, Edward was so impressed with Coucy that the ruler allowed him to regain

vertländischen Geschichte. Neue Folge 2 (1888), pp.113–124.

2 Justinger, *Die Berner-Chronik,* pp.126–128 and Etterlin, Petermann. *Kronica von der loblichen Eidgnossenschaft* (Basel: Daniel Eckenstein, 1752), pp.90–91.

3 Justinger, *Die Berner-Chronik,* pp.133–136 and Eduard von Wattenwyl von Diesbach, *Geschichte der Stadt und Landschaft Bern: Dreizehntes Jahrhundert* (Schaffhausen: Hurter, 1867), pp.196–202.

4 Barbara W. Tuchman, *A Distant Mirror: The Calamitous 14th Century* (New York: Alfred A. Knopf, 1978), p.270.

control over his ancestral lands in England. The king also arranged the marriage of his daughter, Isabella, to Coucy, thus bringing the Frenchman into the English royal family.[5]

In addition to his holdings in England, Coucy had legitimate claims on the Habsburg-owned Aargau bordering the Swiss lands due to the failure of that Austrian noble house to meet the agreements in the marriage contract of his mother. His interest in leading these troops was also enhanced by the fact that he could perhaps gain control of family lands in and near the Swiss Cantons. Coucy was the son of Katharina von Habsburg or Catherine of Austria (1320–1349), whose father, Leopold I von Habsburg (ca. 1290–1326), had been so severely defeated at the Battle of Morgarten. Katharina's dowry was supposed to have included a payment of 8,000 silver marks, while the towns in the Aargau including Sempach, Sursee, Aarau, Lenzburg, and Bremgarten were promised to her if the sum was not paid. Neither was the amount paid nor was there a transfer of the towns made to her control, and part of the reason why Coucy marched into the Swiss lands was to recoup the funds owed him or to get control of these towns.[6]

Cavalry, including mounted crossbowman. Diebold Schilling the Elder, *Spiezer Chronik*, approx. 1484/1485. (Bern. Burgerbibliothek, Mss.h.h.I.16)

Coucy's army consisted of both French and English troops, but the fame of the yeomen led the Swiss sources to believe that the entire army was composed entirely of Englishmen. The people called the invaders *Gugler* after their helmets that came to a dull point at the top similar to a monk's hood. The *Gugler* came in such numbers that the usually believable figures presented by the Swiss sources were clearly inflated. Justinger wrote that the number was 80,000 cavalry, but he did not comment on the infantry.[7] The *Chronik der Stadt Zürich* reported that there were 300,000 (*dri mal hundert tusent*) invaders on horseback and on foot.[8] While modern scholars have reduced the numbers considerably, their estimates still range widely. The prominent Swiss historian, Karl Dändliker, has given the figure of about 50,000 men, and Tuchman has made an estimate of 10,000 troops based on the number of captains leading the army.[9] The figures which the chroniclers gave were so inordinately high that the *Gugler* may have come in incomprehensible numbers, or these accounts reflected the terror the people felt facing the much-feared English.

5 Tuchman, *A Distant Mirror*, pp.195 and 207.
6 Dändliker, *Geschichte der Schweiz*, vol. 1, p.547.
7 Justinger, *Die Berner-Chronik*, p.141.
8 *Chronik der Stadt Zürich*, Johannes Dierauer (ed.) (Basel: Adolf Geering, 1900), pp.83–84.
9 Dändliker, *Geschichte der Schweiz*, vol. 1, p.547 and Tuchman, *A Distant Mirror*, p.271.

The army marched through Champagne in July 1375, to Lorraine in August, and then they invaded Alsace, which was owned by the Habsburgs, in September.[10] Their march through Alsace was marked by destruction. They 'destroyed villages and did damage both to people and property.'[11] The army had a very bad reputation, and the chronicler, Justinger, spared no derisive terms in describing them. They were comprised of 'murderers, robbers, arsonists, those who break into churches, rapists, those who make disasters, torturers, and many evildoers.' The army was in Alsace from 29 September until 11 November 1375 where these forces captured many small cities which they burned. The troops, in their effort for full destruction, reportedly also cut down trees, which certainly required much heavy labour. The peasants had no choice but to flee into the larger cities for greater protection in order to survive. The invaders also destroyed cloisters, churches, and chapels.[12]

The largest city of Alsace, Strasbourg, took in many refugees fleeing the soldiers, but that urban centre felt forced to pay the invaders a heavy ransom to get them to leave the area. The army then advanced on Basel, which had a strong connection with the Swiss Confederation, even though the city would only become a full member of the alliance in 1501, over a century later.

The English immediately threatened the Habsburgs and their holdings, and Duke Leopold III (1351–1386) tried to acquire all the aid possible to repel the invaders. Despite the deepest animosity from the members of the Confederation, he was able to get Bern and Zurich to sign a short-term pact against Coucy's army. But the treaty was insufficient motivation for any of its signatories to meet the invaders, and no army from those cantons was sent to oppose them.[13]

After ravaging Alsace and advancing past Basel, the Gugler marched into the Aargau which was located between the cantons of Zurich, Lucerne, and Bern. The terrible reputation of the invaders followed them, and they were again described as the most detestable of troops who wantonly burned churches and monasteries. They also burned Waldenburg and Willisau, which were far apart, and all the lands between them. Bern had trouble deciding on a course of action. The Bernese sent an army to meet the enemy, but they soon changed their minds, and they recalled their troops. Meeting little resistance, the invaders began to destroy and plunder the countryside within and without the limits of the Aargau, forcing many to flee for safety in the best-protected towns and cities. Finally, some vigorous action was taken, not as a matter of government policy by the large members of the Confederation, but by the citizens of the areas most threatened, who acted

---

10 Tuchman, *A Distant Mirror*, p.270.

11 *Chronik der Stadt Zürich*, p.84.

12 Justinger, *Die Berner-Chronik*, p.141.

13 *Amtliche Sammlung der ältern Eidgenössische Abschiede* 8 vols. (Lucern: Wener'sche Buchdruckerei, 1861–1874) 1, p.55. Hereafter cited as *Eidgenössische Abschiede*.

without official sanction. These were the 'village people' (*dorflüte*) from the lands of the Nidau, the Aarburg, and Laupen.[14]

The Gugler had come in November of 1375, and the cold weather soon restricted their activities, so they were forced to seek shelter wherever possible. On Christmas night 1375, peasants from Bern and the Aargau heard about the expedition planned by the men from the Nidau, Aarburg, and Laupen and joined them. Then they all marched on Ins in the Canton of Bern to surprise the enemy in their sleep. The peasants threw their adversaries into a panic, and the attackers pursued the invaders, stabbing and killing them as they fled. Little effective resistance was offered as 300 men were cut down.[15]

Encouraged by this success, the peasants carried out a nearly identical operation on the following evening at the monastery at Fraubrunnen. Marching through the cold, with the probable aid of torches to light their way, the Bernese and Aargauer peasants again surprised the Gugler. With the Bernese war cry of '*Hie Bern!*' the invaders were awakened and 800 of them were killed, including lords, knights, and servants. These men were killed either by being cut down or by being burned alive when some buildings were set on fire. The peasants captured three banners belonging to the Gugler, which were taken as prizes to Bern. The attackers also seized a great deal of materials including horses, suits of armour, money, clothing, and jewels. Only a few of the Bernese were killed, including Jans Rieder and 'Tall Heinrich,' (*gross heini*). At about the same time, the peasants attacked the Gugler at Buttisholtz in a similar surprise move, which also led to the slaughter of the invaders.[16]

For the price of only three or four Bernese fatalities, the peasants had accomplished a considerable achievement. A much-feared army became uneasy about its position, realised that it could not maintain itself in the wintertime in the Aargau, and withdrew. Surely, the apparent lack of housing, and perhaps the small food supply had much to do with the decision. However, food and shelter were available if the fortified towns could have been taken and foraging parties were sent out once again, but the Christmas action of the local peasants had convinced the Gugler that the price of accomplishing these activities would have been too high.

Both night time operations and winter campaigns were rare in this era. The success of each depended on a sure knowledge of the area and also the skilful use of timing. Each movement was well-conceived and executed, showing that the Swiss had impressive abilities. While the exact composition of the forces involved is unknown, these troops surely came largely from unimportant towns and villages and were members of the

14 Justinger, *Die Berner-Chronik,* p.143.

15 Justinger, *Die Berner-Chronik,* p.143.

16 Justinger, *Die Berner-Chronik,* pp.143–144, Etterlin, *Kronica von der loblichen Eidgnossenschaft*, pp.91–94, and *Klingenberger Chronik*, Anton Henne von Sargans, ed. (Gotha: Parthes, 1861), pp.104–106.

lower classes acting without official sanction. This shows that there was a considerable military expertise among the commoners and peasants which could be used when the proper motivation was present. These abilities also were demonstrated when the Swiss were well organised and at war with official sanction.

6

The Battle of Sempach, 9 July 1386

Background to War

When the Gugler retreated, and threat of invasion from them had been removed, the old animosities between the Habsburgs and the Swiss Confederation soon led to renewed conflict. Clearly, the war of Swiss independence had never been concluded. The Habsburgs had never been able to avenge the losses they suffered at the Battle of Morgarten, because they had been occupied in a conflict with Louis the Bavarian. For his part, Louis was supportive of the independence of the Forest Cantons, and he had issued official decrees to that effect. The Habsburgs never concluded a formal peace treaty with the Forest Cantons, and an open state of hostility existed since the entry of Zurich into the Swiss Confederation in 1351, even though both sides had agreed to a series of armistices which were renewed year after year. However, the two sides were never totally at peace, and latent animosities sometimes caused hostilities to break out. Yet even in times of relative peace, the new members of the Confederation took numerous opportunities to consolidate their positions and even to expand their territory.[1] Lucerne was aggressive at this time, and it took the small town of Sempach under its control on 6 January 1386.

In the last half of the fourteenth century, many towns, cities, and rural areas developed in France, Germany, and Switzerland, and they began to compete for autonomy and control of their affairs. To do so, these communities and regions had to push out the noble factions, to severely limit their authority, or to destroy them. These areas included Bern, Lucerne, and the Forest Cantons in the Swiss areas. This effort was aided by the fact that the higher social classes in many areas were in decline. Many of the nobles of Burgundy and Germany were impoverished by a lack of

1 Delbrück, *Geschichte der Krieskunst*, vol. 3, pp.[598]–599.

money because the income from their holdings no longer met the needs of their relatively lavish lifestyle, and they were forced to sell or mortgage many of their manors, fortresses, and castles.

In February 1386, the Swiss Confederation and Austria negotiated yet another truce that was scheduled to last until 17 June 1386. By then, both sides seemed to hope that many of the differences between them could be settled without conflict, but the agreement between the Swiss and the Empire's cities for a continued peace collapsed. The failure of the efforts for a favourable treaty to both sides was understandable because many issues were still in dispute. Unfortunately, these points of contention had to be settled by war.

When the truce expired in mid-June 1386, the feuds broke out again. Austria's interests were supported by a major faction of nobles, and more than 150 Lords and Princes sent the Swiss Confederation letters announcing their refusal to renew the truce. The Swiss cantons believed that Duke Leopold III (1351–1386) would then resume his attempts to subdue Zurich, which had loosened its association with the Austrians after joining the Confederation in 1351. Therefore, the Swiss sent a garrison to protect and defend the city, and they undertook forays into the Austrian areas where they burned and plundered. On one of these expeditions, the Swiss went into the lands formerly controlled by the Kyburgs, and they plundered and burned the village of Pfäffikon, but they left the nearby fortress undamaged. On other occasions, the Swiss took and burned the small towns of Bülach and Rümlang north of Zurich and harvested their grain. Yet the Austrians were hardly innocent, and they did as much damage as they could in return. Both parties lit up the entire area with small-scale raids.

In the meantime, Leopold assembled an Austrian army. The Duke got contingents from Alsace, the Breisgau Valley, Swabia, the Thurgau, the Aargau, and Burgundy, and Leopold personally marched with his men through the Aargau.[2] He also sent a smaller division of his forces from Brugg to Baden that appeared to threaten Zurich. In this manner, he

Heavy cavalryman armed with lance. Bendicht Tschachtlan, Heinrich Dittlinger, *Tschachtlanchronik*, Bern, 1470. (Zentralbibliothek Zürich, Ms A 120)

2 Dändliker, *Geschichte der Schweiz*, vol. 1, pp.565–566.

seemed to be trying to confuse the Confederates as to his plans. He wanted them to believe that the main attack would be against Zurich when he was planning to move on Sempach, and that town could have been a staging area to assemble forces to march on Lucerne. The men of the Forest Cantons seemed to have guessed Leopold's intentions, so they withdrew their forces from Zurich and went home to better prepare for the real nature of the threat.

At the same time, Leopold marched with his forces from Brugg to Zofingen. From that position, he sent a contingent of men to besiege Willisau, which capitulated on 30 June 1386, and Leopold and his army occupied the town starting on 1 July 1386 where they remained for one week. Apparently, Leopold wanted to take and punish the town of Sempach, which had been disloyal to him. At least, the Confederates thought so, and Lucerne sent a garrison to Sempach to help in the defence of the position. A force of Lucerners and other Confederates marched to lay siege to Sursee, but the Duke and his men left Wallisau and drove the Swiss back to Sempach.[3]

When Leopold left Wallisau on 8 July 1386, he set the small city on fire. He spent that night in Sursee. He then marched the next day, Monday 9 July 1386, on Sempach. Apparently, he was not thinking about engaging in battle that day, since all his forces had yet to assemble. Perhaps the men on foot and the lighter troops had been sent to besiege Sempach directly, while Leopold and his knights deployed on some high ground to the east to hold back a possible relief army from Lucerne.[4]

The Opposing Forces

The earliest sources on the number of Leopold's forces were very consistent. According to Justinger, they numbered, 'perhaps 3,000 armed men.' 'over 4,000,' 'The enemy [Leopold's army] had been indeed 4,000 men on horse and on foot.'[5] The chronicler, Petermann Etterlin, wrote that there were '4,000 on horseback and on foot'[6] Wernher Schodeler, another early source, stated that the numbers were 'More than 4,000 on horseback and on foot' (*mehr dann vier thusend gewesen zu ross und fuss*).[7] Another chronicler, Heinrich Brennwald, wrote that there were 'over 4,000 men on horseback as well as men on foot'[8] Hans Füsslin, an early source, wrote that the number was

3 Dändliker, *Geschichte der Schweiz*, vol. 1, p.567.
4 Dändliker, *Geschichte der Schweiz*, vol. 1, p.568.
5 Justinger, *Die Berner-Chronik*, p.163.
6 Etterlin as cited in Theodor von Liebenau (ed.) *Die Schlacht bei Sempach Gedenkbuch zur fünften Säcularfeier*. (Luzern: C. F. Prell, 1886), p.207. Hereafter cited as Liebenau, *Sempach*.
7 Wernher Schodeler in Liebenau, *Sempach*, p.215.
8 Brennwald in Liebenau, *Sempach*, p.233.

also '4,000 well-armed men.'[9] Hans Delbrück, the eminent German military historian, has again proposed numbers stating that the Swiss outnumbered their adversaries. He asserted that Leopold's army at Sempach was 3,000 or maybe 4,000, while the Swiss were somewhere between 6,000 and 8,000 men.[10] Delbrück's numbers fail to be supported in any of the early accounts on the battle and are clearly absurd.

Much more reliable numbers on the size of the Swiss forces were presented in the most dependable sources. Jakob Twinger von Königshofen stated that the men from Lucerne, Uri, Schwyz and Unterwalden understood Leopold's intentions, and they sent 2,000 armed men on foot, but the men from Bern and Zurich were not with them.[11] The *Zürcher-Chronik* from the early fifteenth century stated that the Confederates numbered not more than 1,500.[12] Justinger stated, that the men from 'Lucerne, Uri, Schwyz, and Unterwalden had 1,300 men.'[13] Johan Viler stated that the duke came with 700 swords (nobles), while the Swiss had 2,000 men.[14] According to Melchior Russ, Uri, Schwyz, Unterwalden, and Lucerne had no more than 300 men each.[15] Petermann Etterlin stated that Uri, Schwyz, Unterwalden

The Battle of Sempach 9 July 1386. Diebold Schilling the Younger, *Eidgenössische Chronik des Luzerners*, Lucerne, 1513. (ZHB Luzern Sondersammlung, S 23 fol.)

9 Füsslin in Liebenau, *Sempach*, p.237.
10 Delbrück, *Geschichte der Krieskunst*, vol. 3, p.599.
11 Twinger in Liebenau, *Sempach*, pp.117–119.
12 *Zürcher Chronik* in Liebenau, *Sempach*, p.150.
13 Justinger, *Die Berner-Chronik*, p.163.
14 Viler in Liebenau, *Sempach*, pp.158–159.
15 Russ in Liebenau, *Sempach*, pp.181–182.

and Lucerne marched with 1,300 men.[16] Brennwald wrote almost the exact same number, and he said Uri, Schwyz, Unterwalden and Lucerne came with 1,300 men.[17] Aegidius Tschudi gave the most detailed description of the forces the Swiss brought to the battle. 'There were up to 1,300 troopers namely 400 from Lucerne, 300 from Uri, 300 from Schwyz, 200 from Unterwalden, and there were also various fighters from Zug and Glarus from Entlibuch and from Rothenburg nearly 100 troopers.'[18] The rough consensus among the early sources was that Duke Leopold had over 4,000 men on horseback as well as men on foot. The men from the Forest Cantons and Lucerne had roughly 1,300 to 1,500 men.

The quality of the men from Uri, Schwyz, Unterwalden, and Lucerne in the battle was very good. As advanced guards from their respective cantons, these contingents would be expected to be the best men available, and their leaders were men of prestige and perceived ability. The leader of Lucerne's forces was Petermann von Gundelingen, who was recognised as a knight, and he also served as mayor of the city. Cunrad der Frowen was a 'bailiff, mayor, and head leader' of the forces from Uri.[19] Additionally, these troops had recently campaigned in support of Zurich, and they had received valuable practice in marching, deployment, and manoeuvres at that time. They would soon test their abilities in desperate battle with Leopold's forces. These troops wore armour typical of the Swiss of the era. The nature of these protective materials was based largely on the wealth of the wearer. Most of the men wore at least leather coverings on their arms, legs, stomach, and chest. The wealthy could often afford more protection including metal breastplates and gloves. Helmets were especially prized because the men were subject to downward slashes from their enemies, and metal protection on their heads would help them survive battle. The weaponry of the Forest Cantons still consisted of short pole weapons including halberds and battle axes, but many of the men from Lucerne wielded a slightly different instrument, the Lucerne hammer or death hammer (*Mordhammer*). This was a device with a shaft roughly four to six feet or up to two metres long with a spear point at the top for thrusting. On one side of the tip, it had a hook for snagging armour, but on the opposite side, it had a three or four pronged head similar to that of a hammer, which could be used to smash armour.[20]

Leopold's forces included a large number of knights, and many of these men were nobles of high status and impressive military prowess. Of the roughly 4,000 men in the Duke's army, 'about 700 were good knights.' These troops were also called '700 swordsmen' (*syben hundert glefen*), meaning

16 Etterlin in Liebenau, *Sempach*, pp.206–207.
17 Brennwald in Liebenau, *Sempach*, pp.233–234.
18 Tschudi in Liebenau, *Sempach*, p.254.
19 Heinrich Bullinger in Liebenau, *Sempach*, p.278.
20 Wendelin Boeheim, *Handbuch der Waffenkunde in seiner historischen Entwickelung von Beginn des Mittelalters bis zum Ende des 18. Jahrhunderts* (Leipzig: Seeman, 1890), p.364.

they were wielding expensive and effective cutting weapons known to be used by the knights.[21] The *glefen* or glaive was often comprised of two or three warriors. If accurate in this case, 700 swords could mean 1,400 to 2,100 men on horseback were with Leopold's army.[22] Many of these men came from the higher levels of the nobility and could be expected to have all the expensive armaments and weapons available. While the sources make little mention of men of foot in the Duke's army, it has long been assumed that 'there was indicated a great number of foot soldiers' with these forces.[23]

Late in the fourteenth century, the protective coverings worn by the knights were undergoing a fundamental shift from chain mail to plate armour in many places in Europe, including the Austrian lands, as skilled armour makers were advancing their craft. Big factors in this shift to plate armour was the increased effectiveness of the crossbow and the impact of the English longbow, which had been very successful in doing significant damage to knights wearing chain mail in the early phases of the Hundred Years' War. While the arrow shot from the longbow or the bolt shot from a crossbow could go through chain mail, plate armour offered more protection against these fearsome weapons. A major drawback to the use of plate armour was the fact that the knight could have extreme problems with heat because there was no means of air to reach the body of the warrior to evaporate his sweat and to cool him. Knights typically wore cloth over their armour, called a surcoat, which was frequently decorated with heraldic symbols, including their coats of arms. These decorations on the fabrics were often used for identification. Yet they also had a small practical value because the cloth reflected some sunlight, so the men would be slightly less hot in their armour.

The Armies Organise for Battle

Duke Leopold marched with his men from Sursee on the morning of 9 July 1386 with the intention of taking Sempach by assault if necessary. The town was defended by the Swiss militia, and these forces had every intention of making the conquest of the town to be very difficult. Consistent with much warfare of the age, which involved much devastation and plunder, the Duke planned to ravage the area if the conquest of the small city proved difficult. His men would then lay waste to all the grain and other crops in the region to cut down everything and leave the Swiss in misery and starvation. To accomplish the work of crop destruction, the Leopold had brought with him 200 reapers with scythes and other equipment to do the work.[24]

21 Twinger in Liebenau, *Sempach*, p.117.

22 Frey, *Kriegstaten der Schweizer*, p.105.

23 Alexander Schweizer, *Eine Studie zur Schlacht bei Sempach 9. Juli 1386* (Zürich: Berichthaus, 1902), p.12.

24 Twinger in Liebenau, *Sempach*, p.117.

When the men from Lucerne, Uri, Schwyz, and Unterwalden learned of the Duke's activities, they sent their armed men on foot to intercept them. These contingents were a relatively small part of the Swiss armies, because the forces from Bern and Zurich were deployed elsewhere. Apparently, Bern was poorly informed of the nature of the threat, and it was concerned about possible incursions into its land. Also, Zurich knew enemy forces were nearby and kept their troops for the protection of the city.[25]

The meeting of the two armies was unexpected by both sides. Leopold had yet to assemble his entire forces, but he decided to give battle anyway obviously believing that he had enough effective manpower to be victorious. Since many of his men were mounted, they could choose to engage or break off military action any time they chose. The Swiss contingents, being on foot, could hardly withdraw unless the Duke's men allowed them to do so. Even though the Swiss also came to battle with less than their full complements of troops, they could hardly run away from horses and had to face whatever their mounted opponents threw at them.

Clearly, Leopold, and at least some of his men, were eager for battle, and some were filled with bravado and disdain for their enemies. As described by an early source, 'The nobility were courageous and joyous because of their great power. [But] they did not remember the saying that overconfidence and contempt for the enemy are unwise' because that could lead to disaster.[26] There were many young nobles in the Duke's army who were still squires and had yet to achieve the status of being dubbed a knight. They wanted to gain that honour by some act of valour on the battlefield, 'And [they] yelled about the Swiss, "Someone should stab the boys to death."'[27]

In the meantime, the Swiss had made their wedge-shaped battle formation (*spitze*), had organised themselves for battle, and had placed themselves in a position to fight.[28] This wedge was some kind of inverted V disposition with the point facing the enemy, and the formation was a tradition the Swiss had used at the Battle of Laupen. Presumably, the best men would be placed near the tip of the formation either to break through the enemy ranks if attacking or to disrupt the opposing forces when the Swiss stood in defence. But the configuration had some serious weaknesses. By necessity, the sides of the wedge had to be relatively long, and the formation would lack depth. This meant that the sides were vulnerable if attacked, especially when men on horseback assaulted them. The Swiss also wielded weapons with short staffs, including halberds and Lucerne hammers, which were less effective in fending off heavy cavalry.

25 Twinger in Liebenau, *Sempach*, p.117.

26 Tschudi in Liebenau, *Sempach*, p.255.

27 Twinger in Liebenau, *Sempach*, p.117. '*unde schrouwent über die Switzer, men solte die bueben erstechen*.'

28 Twinger in Liebenau, *Sempach*, p.117.

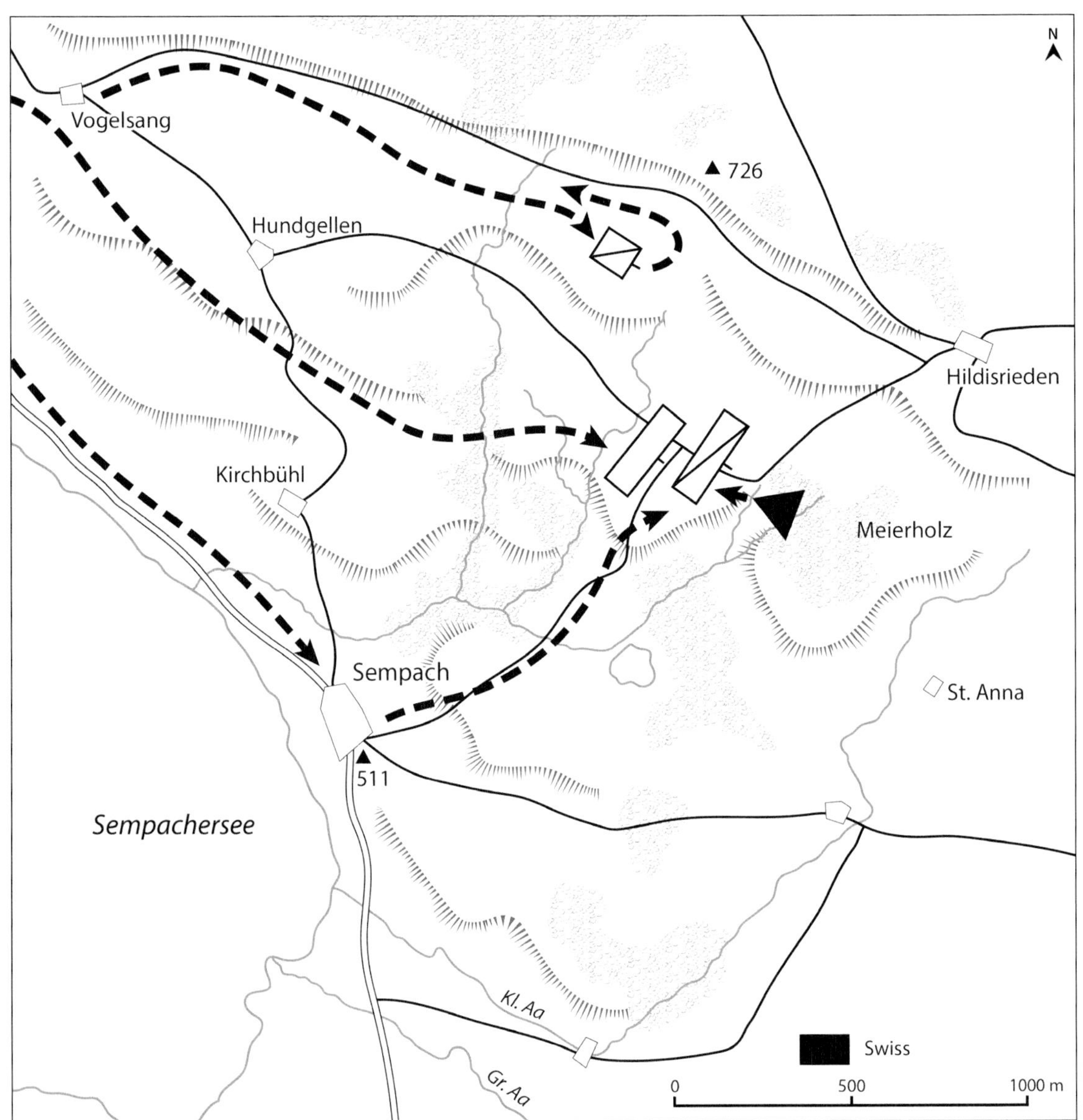

The Battle of Sempach, 9 July 1386

Leopold's Decision to Dismount

Leopold and his men enjoyed considerable advantages as knights on horseback, but the Duke gave away these favourable circumstances when he ordered his men to dismount and fight on foot, which had disastrous consequences. The decision was most curious, but it was hardly unique because other mounted armies within this time frame also decided to fight on foot. The most famous example would be when the French knights dismounted to fight on foot at the Battle of Agincourt in 1415, with an equally tragic outcome. Recently, historians have argued that the men in the heavy cavalries of that age made the choice to dismount when they thought there were advantages in doing so, such as to meet challenging conditions of the terrain. While fighting on foot had certain advantages in a defensive role, there was no logical condition, whether it be the lay of the land or the abundance of soggy soil, in which advancing on foot would be better than attacking on horseback. The only advantage the foot soldier would have over a man on horseback was if he were climbing a very steep cliff, and that was certainly not the case at Sempach. That battlefield was on a low hill with a modest gradient. Horses are powerful and strong animals, and they can overcome every obstacle much easier than a man on foot especially when the man on foot was wearing heavy armour. These animals were highly effective in attacking the enemy and equally in securing retreat when withdrawal was necessary.

The reason why Leopold had his men dismount may have to do with his concern that some of his troops might run away on horseback if they had the opportunity to do so. Apparently, the Duke's forces were in multiple formations, and one of these groups fled from the battle before it even started. As one of the earliest accounts of the battle stated, 'Afterwards the noble ruler (*Fürst*) heard a piteous yell. "Oh, save yourselves, Austrians, run for your lives!"' In reaction to the flight of some of his men, the Duke took definitive action. 'The courageous ruler [Leopold] called to all his knights and squires that they, together with him, [should] dismount from their horses and save [the fleeing] knights and squires.' Additionally, 'The noble ruler [Leopold] got down from his horse and marched against the enemy very gallantly with his loyal knights and squires just as would a lion.'[29]

The knights and their squires were ill-prepared to fight on foot, and their clothing and armour were designed for use on horseback. The largest single problem was their shoes. The footwear worn by knights was called the sabaton. Fashion at the time of the battle meant that these boots were poulaines, which had very long pikes or beaks on their toes, somewhat similar to a bird's beak or bill. This footwear was ungainly to say the least, and these boots would inhibit a trooper's ability to walk and therefore fight on the ground. They simply had to be altered or removed. As one early

---

29 Hagen in Liebenau, *Sempach*, p.113.

source stated, 'Then the nobles prepared for battle on foot, and they cut off the points of their shoes.'[30] Another source stated that the Duke had his men get down from their horses, because he wanted them to fight on foot. Many men followed that order. They dismounted for battle as did their squires, and they were described as 'the most manly and trustworthy knights and squires who were in this land.'[31] They then hacked off the pointed ends of their shoes.[32]

While these men could still be very effective on the ground, the knights were still clearly out of their element on foot. The fact that they had to alter their shoes meant that they had never practiced fighting on the ground, and they suffered other disadvantages. Their helmets were designed for men on horseback, and their eye slits were adequate in that environment, because they usually faced their adversaries from the front. Yet these same eye slits limited vision for men on the ground who often needed to meet threats from every direction. Additionally, the knights knew very little about the best ways to wield their weapons on foot or how to form advantageous formations in that environment. The old supposition that men fully encased in plate armour were ungainly or awkward has been fully debunked by modern research. Clearly, the knights could run and manoeuvre very well wearing that protection, but their lack of experience meant they still knew little about how to pace themselves to keep from becoming exhausted or overheated. This potential problem was especially true because a full suit of mail armour or plate armour would often weigh from 45 to 55 pounds (20 to 25 kilograms).

Battlefield at Sempach in 1386. Diebold Schilling the Younger, *Eidgenössische Chronik des Luzerners*, Lucerne, 1513. (ZHB Luzern Sondersammlung, S 23 fol.)

There was another potential detriment when the knights dismounted. Someone had to hold the horses while the men advanced on foot. They got down 'off their horses and gave them to their squires to hold.'[33] If these attendants had been among those young men who wanted to gain knighthood by some act of valour on the battlefield, then holding the horses would have taken possible combatants away from the battle, thus depleting the Duke's army. Each squire could have held more than one horse, but the number would have been limited. Assuming that they held the same number of mounts as did the US Cavalry during the Indian Wars of the nineteenth century, then each attendant would be expected to hold four horses. If so, perhaps the total strength of the Duke's forces of men from the class of knights could have been reduced

30 Füsslin in Liebenau, *Sempach*, p.237.
31 *Thurgauer-Chronik* in Liebenau, *Sempach*, p.130.
32 Tschudi in Liebenau, *Sempach*, p.253.
33 Twinger in Liebenau, *Sempach*, p.117. '*von iren hengesten und gobent die iren knechten ze habende*.'

by as much as one quarter. Yet the men assigned to hold the horses could have also comprised a battle formation, and 'the Swartz [black] Count von Zolrn and Lord Johannes von Oberkilch, a knight, with a number of men on horseback and on foot, were ordered into a rearguard.'[34] This made good sense if these troops were to be deployed as a supplement to the forces perhaps at a critical juncture in the battle. Yet they later failed to respond as needed, and their number was effectively removed from Leopold's combat troops.

The Austrian Advance

Often, the leaders of armies stayed behind their men when engaged in battle perhaps to direct the contest better or to escape the chance of being killed, and some of the Duke's men thought that he should do the same. 'Then they said to Duke Leopold that he should not fight, [but] he should stand still and see how everyone conducted themselves and let them do the fighting.' He refused to take the precaution, and 'the pious ruler' said, 'God does not want that.' He added, 'Should I leave you to die, and I survive?' In another version of Leopold's comments, he referred to his family's honour.[35] 'God does not want that. Should I let you die and I be safe? I will face the good and bad with you. I will stay by my knights and squires and will either live or die according to my personal heritage and that of my family.'[36]

Another version of the story stated that the Duke reacted when a few of his men began to run away at the beginning of the battle rather than fight. 'Some, however, got on their horses and began to flee. A few thought that the prince should join them and save his life.' Yet Leopold said, 'He would rather die with honour than live on Earth without it.' The Duke's performance in battle was impressive. 'And he fought against the enemy with all his loyal knights and squires and killed many enemies, and the enemy prevailed and won. And the praiseworthy Prince's [Leopold's] spirit was recommended to the hands of God.'[37]

The sources present a discrepancy on how Leopold's army approached the Swiss forces. Some said that the Austrians were in some state of disarray, 'and they hurried in disorder (*ungeordet*) one after the other against the Swiss.'[38] Also, 'They marched together with each other not in good order'[39] Additionally, they 'formed no wedge (*spiez*) nor an order among them. … Rather they hurried one after the other.'[40] The Austrians advancing in

34 Tschudi in Liebenau, *Sempach*, p.255.
35 *Thurgauer-Chronik* in Liebenau, *Sempach*, p.130.
36 Tschudi in Liebenau, *Sempach*, p.253.
37 Haben in Liebenau, *Sempach*, p.113.
38 Twinger in Liebenau, *Sempach*, p.117.
39 *Thurgauer-Chronik* in Liebenau, *Sempach*, p.130.
40 Blasianer in Liebenau, *Sempach*, p.140.

a complete state of disorder was surprising and perhaps highly unlikely. The only chance the Duke's army had to assault the Swiss effectively would have been to stand close together. If the men had been separated, their effectiveness would have been limited, and each could have been easily surrounded by several enemies and killed even if they came 'one after another.' Since Leopold's men did severe damage to the Swiss early in the engagement, there must have been in some kind of tight formation, and the early sources disagree on this topic. 'They [the Austrians] made themselves into a good, strong order, and they stationed the great nobles at the point of a wedge-shaped formation.'[41]

A quaint story tells of how the Swiss reacted when they saw Leopold's army approach. 'When the Swiss saw their enemy, they fell onto their knees and prayed with outstretched arms, which was their custom.' When the enemy saw this, they ridiculed the Swiss saying, 'The fearful men have fallen down on their knees asking us for mercy [on them].' This clearly indicated that no compassion would be given. But the Confederates stood up and advanced toward the enemy from the forest. The Duke then got news of this movement and called his men to battle.[42]

The Austrian Attack

The Duke's forces were stationed near the top of an incline, and they were able to attack down the slope, which gave them a slight advantage in momentum. An early account of the initial contact between the armies stated, 'Then the nobles came down from the mountain with a great shout and threw stones and with a hard attack' that struck the Confederates hard.'[43] Some sources state that Leopold's army advanced down from the 'mountain' (*den Berg herab*), but that was an exaggeration. A personal examination of the battlefield has shown that the Austrians were on higher ground, but the slope of the terrain would hardly be considered steep, so it is better to state that the Duke's men came down from a hill. But the lay of the land might have been significantly different in the Middle Ages because farming techniques, especially the use of the plough, would have levelled much of the terrain over the centuries. If so, Leopold's men might have made good use of the momentum provided from gravity, especially if they advanced at a quick step or on the run. Also, the statement that the nobles entered the battle by throwing stones is also suspect. This tactic was used by the Swiss, but it was largely unknown among the nobles who enjoyed more sophisticated weapons, and they also would have trouble flinging rocks when their arms were encased in armour.

---

41 Tschudi in Liebenau, *Sempach*, p.255.
42 Tschudi in Liebenau, *Sempach*, p.254.
43 *Zürcher Chronik* in Liebenau, *Sempach*, p.162.

The impetus of the nobles was impressive, and they cut their way into the Swiss ranks. 'Surely 60 men [Swiss] were killed before anything happened to the nobles.' Apparently, this meant that 60 Swiss were cut down before a single nobleman fell. There is no way to know if such a precise number was correct, but the account clearly indicated that the knights were very successful in the first stages of the battle. The earliest narrative account of the battle also praises the Duke's men's success in the early phase of the contest.[44] 'And [Leopold] fought against the enemy with all his loyal knights and squires and killed many enemy.' The sources often praise the fighting of both the knights and the Swiss stating that each side fought courageously and 'knightly' (*ritterleich*).[45] Also, the battle 'was fought knightly (*ritterlich*) by both sides.'[46]

The nobles pressed their attack deep into the Swiss formations to the point that 'the banner of Lucerne went down because of great adversity.'[47] The canton's flag or banner was often placed in the centre of their formation, so the men could see where they should stand in relation to it, and the emblem was also defended by the strongest and most able men. When a banner fell, it meant that the most important position in the battle order was taken, and the entire battle disposition was on the verge of collapse. This usually meant that the formation had been defeated, and the battle was all but lost. In fact, the Swiss were beginning to crack, and some ran away to save their lives. As one source stated, 'The battle was so long that some of the Confederates started to flee.'[48]

Apparently, 200 men from Lucerne fled from the field of battle at about the same time as their city banner fell, clearly leaving their allies at a severe disadvantage as the fight continued. Fortunately, the other Swiss were able to continue the fight, but this example of cowardice had a lengthy impact on these men's reputation. The city officials of Lucerne did not formally punish them, but the citizens called them 'the women of Sempach' (*die Weiber von Sempach*) for the rest of their lives. This term of disgrace also fell upon the descendants of these men for the next three generations.[49]

The issue of possible cowardice in the battle was a serious matter, and it even came up in a court case in 1417 in Lucerne over 30 years after the conflict. At that time, Werne Güpfer made a public accusation that Heinrich Tripscher 'had fled from the field at [the battle of] Sempach (*geflochen vor Sempach*). Therefore, he and his child [son] could never hold a position of authority in Lucerne nor in the city council.' The issue was so important that it was taken to the council of 100 for a decision. The outcome of the

44 *Zürcher Chronik* in Liebenau, *Sempach*, p.162.
45 Hagen in Liebenau, *Sempach*, p.113.
46 Twinger in Liebenau, *Sempach*, p.117.
47 *Zürcher Chronik* in Liebenau, *Sempach*, p.162.
48 Füsslin in Liebenau, *Sempach*, p.237.
49 Bruno Hübscher, *Die Entwicklung und Struktur des Luzernischen Heerwesens von 1291–1500*. (Hochdorf: Buchdrückerei Hochdorf, 1943), p.39.

Swiss infantry at Sempach in 1386. Diebold Schilling the Younger, *Eidgenössische Chronik des Luzerners*, Lucerne, 1513. (ZHB Luzern Sondersammlung, S 23 fol.)

inquest was unclear because men named Tripscher were known to have served in civic affairs after this time, but they may have been brothers of Heinrich.[50]

The Swiss corpses began to pile up. 'They [the nobles] were cheerful and undeterred. In the assault, they beat the Confederates hard and struck many of them dead so that a great mass of lifeless Swiss was heaped up in front of the nobles.'[51] The knights had done severe damage to their enemies, but the Swiss continued to resist. The fact that so many of the Swiss were piled up meant that they had been making some kind of a stand. If they had broken and fled, then the corpses would have been scattered all over the battlefield, but clearly a crisis had been reached, and victory or defeat for both sides hung in the balance.

The Swiss Hold and Winkelried's Deed

At this critical juncture in the battle, a courageous man apparently made a difference. 'Then a true man of the Confederates helped us.' This man saw that everything was going poorly for the Swiss, and that the nobles were stabbing men to death with their pikes before the Confederates could properly drive forward with their halberds. 'Then the honourable and pious man dived forward and seized as many pikes as he could grab and pushed them down so that the Confederates could cut off the pikes with their halberds, and then they (the Swiss) came after them [the enemy]' clearly to press the attack.[52] Certainly, the unnamed man had taken enough weapons out of the hands of the enemy by grabbing and falling on them, so that the Swiss were able to press the attack through the gap he made and turn the tide of battle.

50 *Plasphemie accusate* in Liebenau, *Sempach*, p.396.
51 *Thurgauer-Chronik* in Liebenau, *Sempach*, p.130.
52 *Zürcher Chronik* in Liebenau, *Sempach*, p.162.

The earliest source on this deed was the *Züricher Chronik*, and it was written about 1438, and this date of composition made it among the earliest accounts of the battle. Sources written roughly one century later added a few details, and they also gave the man's name as Arnold von Winkelried, a resident of a distinguished family in Unterwalden.[53] It must be noted that a man named Erni Winckelrieth from Underwalden ob dem Wald (part of Unterwalden) was listed among the dead in the Swiss books of yearly commemoration for the battle.[54] While the earliest source of his deed failed to mention that he had been killed as a result of his action, that consequence would hardly have been surprising. The later sources made his demise clear. It was also added that he had called to his fellow Swiss just before he jumped on the enemy spears and sacrificed his life, 'Care, dear Confederates, for my wife and children.'

The question of the authenticity of Winkelried's deed has sparked controversy among historians going back to the nineteenth century, and some were willing to place the story very much within the same category as Wilhelm Tell's supposed actions and dismiss it as a legend. Even so, some prominent Swiss historians have accepted the story as accurate including Karl Dändliker and the highly respected Johannes von Müller.[55]

Winkelried's deed was certainly plausible, and other well-attested actions in Swiss history describe the same kind of courage including Heini Wolleb's action at the Battle of Frastanz in 1499. Wolleb was a Swiss leader who came from Uri. At a critical juncture in the battle, he rushed forward and pushed up the pikes of his enemies allowing his men to advance through the gap he had formed and gain the victory. In this case, Wolleb was either stabbed to death or shot through the neck and killed.[56]

The account of Winkelried calling to his fellow troops to look after his family in case he was killed could easily be true. Men who go into battle or into other dangerous situations often think about their families and loved ones in case they are killed, and it is common for them to ask others to care for them. It would be expected that many men in the Swiss army would do exactly as did Winkelried and ask his fellow countrymen to help his dependents if he was killed.

The issue of Winkelried's courage and sacrifice may go far beyond the actions of one man in the battle. In fact, Winkelried's bravery may be a simple personification of the actions taken by many others. There can be no doubt that many men in the Swiss army stood their ground and fought to the death rather than give way to the assault by the Duke's men. Their individual acts may not have been as spectacular as grabbing enemy spears

53 Delbrück, *Geschichte der Krieskunst*, vol. 3, pp.603–609.

54 Bullinger in Liebenau, *Sempach*, p.279.

55 Dändliker, *Geschichte der Schweiz*, vol. 1, p.573 and Johannes von Müller, *Sämmtliche Werke*, 27 vols. (Tübingen: J.G. Cotta, 1810–1819) vol. 4, p.57.

56 Albert Winkler, *The Swabian War of 1499: The first Confrontation between Landsknechts and the Swiss* (Warwick: Helion & Company, 2024), p.72.

and then falling on them, but their deeds required an equal amount of determination and courage, and their conduct was equally praiseworthy. Whatever were their names, and no matter where they came from, they contributed significantly to the victory.

The Swiss Counterattack

The courage of the Swiss was only one factor in the outcome of the battle, and many sources described the heat of the day and smothering effect of the knights' armour. As an early source explained, 'Now at that time, it was the hottest day of the year. And in the heat and work in the battle, the nobles soon became wounded and weak so that they began to suffocate in their armour.'[57] Another early source explained some of the problems, 'But the nobles were so burdened with coats and armour that they could not long drive forward. It was a very hot day, and many of the men would have gladly worn less armour. They wavered. Then the Swiss severely counterattacked, and many of the men suffocated from the heat.'[58]

The battle seemed to take place in the afternoon, the hottest time of day. Even though the two armies possibly saw each other early in the day, it took hours for the forces to assemble, to prepare for battle, and to engage each other. The knights had little or no experience fighting on foot, and they had scant knowledge of how to pace themselves, conserve their energy, or to keep from being overcome by the heat. The problem was severe both for men wearing plate armour or chain mail. Plate armour could not allow heat to escape, and the problem was much the same with chain mail because of the thick padding under this armour would also trap body heat. The only place for heat to escape was through the visor of the knights' helmets, but this was completely inadequate. Also, the visors were certainly down for better protection in the intensity of battle thus trapping more heat. Each helmet had to have holes in it to allow the men to breathe, but the openings were often quite small to allow for better protection. The trade-off was the fact that the small holes meant the knights had restricted means of breathing, so their ability to expiate body heat by gasping for air was inhibited. These problems were usually manageable when the knights were on horseback, but when the men were on foot, they could be catastrophic.

Infantry clash. Diebold Schilling the Younger, *Eidgenössische Chronik des Luzerners*, Lucerne, 1513. (ZHB Luzern Sondersammlung, S 23 fol.)

57 Twinger in Liebenau, *Sempach*, p.118.

58 *Thurgauer-Chronik* in Liebenau, *Sempach*, p.130.

When the Swiss noticed that their enemies were becoming weaker as they lost their impetus, the Confederates saw their opportunity to go on the offensive and turn the tide of battle. Presumably at least some of the Duke's men had already collapsed from heat exhaustion before the Swiss struck back, and the remainder had lost much of their strength and were unable to continue the fight. Their situation soon became desperate, and they badly needed immediate support from the only source available, the men holding their horses. If the knights and squires holding the horses and forming the rear guard had engaged the Swiss, there was still a possibility that the contest could have turned in their favour, or at least, the exhausted knights might have a chance to reach their horses and escape. The knights called in desperation. 'Then some of the nobles broke off the fight and called to their squires: "[Bring the] Horses here!"' (*hengst har*! or *hengst her*!)[59] But their cries proved to be in vain, and the knights on foot received no help because the men forming the rear guard panicked and ran away taking the horses with them. 'Then it happened that the Count von Zolrn and the Lord Hans von Oberkilchen and many troops did not engage in the battle but rode away.'[60] This action clearly left the men on foot to their fate, and they were in a desperate situation. Few of them would survive.

The Swiss saw their advantage and staged a counterattack. 'Soon the Confederates left their wedge-shaped battle formation and attacked (ran after) the nobles and struck so dreadfully with the halberds that nothing could withstand the slashing. Quickly, God gave the Confederates good fortune that they were victorious and claimed the field of battle with great honour.'[61] Many of the knights were clearly killed by the Swiss slashing with their halberds 'And then many counts, knights, squires and nobles were battered to death.' The number of dead nobles included Duke Leopold who seemed to have died in the midst of the battle. At least some of the knights were able to flee as far as the trees to their rear before they were killed. 'And many men were found dead in the forest, and many others were also stabbed to death.'[62]

Infantry equipped with different types of polearms. Diebold Schilling the Younger, *Eidgenössische Chronik des Luzerners*, Lucerne, 1513. (ZHB Luzern Sondersammlung, S 23 fol.)

59 Blasianer in Liebenau, *Sempach*, p.140.

60 *Thurgauer-Chronik* in Liebenau, *Sempach*, p.130 and Twinger in Liebenau, *Sempach*, p.118.

61 Justinger, *Die Berner-Chronik*, p.163.

62 *Zürcher Chronik* in Liebenau, *Sempach*, pp.162–163. See also Twinger in Liebenau, *Sempach*, pp.117–118.

In their thirst for victory, the Swiss took no prisoners but killed every enemy they could catch or find. They certainly knew that every noble or man of high station taken as a prisoner could be ransomed for a great deal of money, and knights were frequently captured whenever possible in Medieval battles or campaigns. Even the lowly squires would have been worth something, and the Swiss surprisingly made no effort to gain wealth through ransom. A practical reason not to take prisoners might have to do with the fact that the battle was yet to be entirely decided, and the men on horses stationed in the rear of the Duke's formation could have made a difference had they engaged in the battle at the right moment. Taking captives might have made the Swiss forces more vulnerable. Yet another factor may have been simple blood lust, and the Confederates were making a statement that any enemy facing them would be treated harshly. If so, they overlooked the fact that the families of the men they cut down might thirst for revenge. All too often, brutality will lead to more atrocities. The Swiss might have also been making a social statement. Most of the Swiss were fighting as free peasants, and they had clear hatred for the upper classes. Perhaps they wanted to treat the privileged stratum the same as they would anyone no matter what their social status.

In battle, relatively few men are killed outright. Even in modern warfare with advanced mechanised killing machines, many more men are wounded than are actually killed in battle. This was presumably true of Medieval warfare where the knights were often encased either in chain mail or in plate armour. Modern experiments have shown that medieval armour, whether it was plate armour or chain mail, was very adept at shielding the wearer from all kinds of weapons including swords, spears, and battle axes. Certainly, knights who were disabled, exhausted, or disarmed on the battlefield were incapable of offering further resistance, but if they were not to be captured, they were to be killed. No source actually stated how these men were dispatched. They could have been battered to death, but this means of killing would require damaging their expensive armour, which was valuable and might be taken as plunder. The most effective way of killing these men would be to stab them either in the arm pit area or in the groin. The armour was thinnest in those areas because the knights needed to have flexibility to sit on their horses and to wield their weapons effectively. Unfortunate for the victims of execution, there are veins and arteries found in those places that could be severed, so the knight would bleed to death.

Battle Casualties

Reports of the casualties suffered by both sides in the battle vary considerably, but the sources agree that the losses were significant. Among the earliest accounts of the conflict was Jakob Twinger, who stated that 'about 200 Swiss were killed. And on the side of the Duke about 400 good men were killed, including great territorial lords and nobles.'[63] If this account has merit, and if the sources which stated that Leopold's army numbered 4,000 and the Swiss forces were about 1,300 to 1,500, then the Swiss lost more men in proportion than did their enemies. But this is far from certain. The *Augsburger Chronik* from 1395 stated that Duke Leopold and 580 counts, knights, and squires were killed.[64] Gregor Hagen stated that Leopold and 250 knights and squires died in the battle.[65]

While most of the accounts on the number of Leopold's men that were killed give general numbers, there are still some specific figures presented. In the *Thurgauer-Chronik* from the early fifteenth century, the author listed the names of the men who fell even 'if they were nobles or non nobles.' Heading the list were 10 important nobles including Duke Leopold. The banner carriers and civic nobles were listed as being 23 in number. There were 37 knights and squires from Swabia as well as 13 nobles and squires from the Etsch area. In addition, there were 31 knights and squires from the upper Alsace, and 22 names of knights and the squires from the Aargau were presented. There were also 13 knights and squires from Basel, 19 from Fribourg, and 14 from Schaffhausen. Also included were 41 from Rheinfelden and other 'cities' for a total of 223.[66]

However, these lists and numbers were far from all those who actually fell, and much larger figures have been presented, including, 'Duke Leopold and 580 counts, knights, squires killed'[67] Also, 'Then fell the Duke of Austria with 676 men.'[68] Another report presented a similar number. 'The Duke lost 666 men.'[69] Estimates went even higher, and one source gave two large numbers in the same sentence. 'On the side of the duke there were 845 men lost, and they lost 1,000 men.'[70] No estimate on the losses suffered by the Duke's army in the battle can ever be satisfactory because the numbers vary considerably. Recent scholarship tends to present relatively modest numbers when it comes to the casualties of medieval battles. Yet the figures of at least 400 to 500 fatalities at the Battle of Sempach, and perhaps more, are reasonable.

As the victorious army, the Swiss losses would be expected to be lower. Yet some Austrian sources still claimed their casualties were high. 'And the Swiss held the field even though 600 of them were killed in this battle.'[71] '200 Swiss were killed.'[72] 'And the Confederates lost 120 men.'[73] 'In this battle

63 Twinger in Liebenau, *Sempach*, p.118.
64 *Augsburger Chronik* in Liebenau, *Sempach*, p.121.
65 Haben in Liebenau, *Sempach*, pp.113–114.
66 *Thurgauer-Chronik* in Liebenau, *Sempach*, pp.131–136.
67 *Augsburger Chronik* in Liebenau, *Sempach*, p.121.
68 *Zürcher Chronik* in Liebenau, *Sempach*, pp.162–163.
69 Dacher in Liebenau, *Sempach*, pp.174–175.
70 *Constanzer-Chronik* in Liebenau, *Sempach*, p.139.
71 *Limburger Chronik* in Liebenau, *Sempach*, p.105.
72 Viler in Liebenau, *Sempach*, p.159.
73 Justinger, *Die Berner-Chronik*, p.163.

no one was taken prisoner and about 200 Swiss were killed.'[74] 'The Swiss lost 102 men.'[75] 'The Swiss lost 300 men.'[76] Other sources give more details on Swiss losses, and one stated that each of the four Swiss Cantons lost 50 men.[77] Another stated that each of the Swiss Cantons lost 50 men, except for Lucerne which lost 51 men. Many men had severe wounds as well as was the case with the Duke's men.[78]

Aegidius (Gilg) Tschudi gave the most detailed account of the Swiss losses. He stated that 116 were killed, but he then gave a list of the names of the fallen, and his total numbers when added together are much higher. He seemed to get his lists of names from the books of 'yearly battle commemoration' (*Schlachtenjahrzeit*) compiled by each of the cantons.[79] The names of the fallen from Lucerne include Petermann von Gundeltingen (or Gundelingen), who was the mayor of the city and Heinrich von Moss, who was a former mayor. The total number of the fatalities from Lucerne was 19. The list of names of the fallen from Uri included Cunrat (or Cunrad) der Frowen, who was a chief magistrate of the canton. Uri suffered 41 fatalities in all. According to Tschudi's account, Schwyz suffered the highest casualties, and this list included 63 names. The canton of 'Nid dem Wald,' or Nidwalden, part of Unterwalden, lost 20 men whose names were presented, and one man from Glarus died. This was a total of 144 men, but certainly other, unnamed, men were also killed.[80] As has been argued, the total losses the Swiss suffered in the battle are also hard to calculate accurately because the numbers presented by the sources vary considerably. Yet estimates of around 200 are reasonable. The lists of names of the fallen, both from the Austrian and Swiss sides, present another layer of reality to the faceless and nameless numbers. These cognomens make the reality of the deaths a little more immediate to us, because they represent real men, and the names of the dead make the tragedy of the losses in the battle all the more disturbing.

The Swiss took many prizes in the battle including 72 major flags and banners (*houptpanner*).[81] The victorious Swiss held the battlefield for three days after the contest, and they removed their dead to their home cantons for burial. They also plundered the area, and they took the expensive armour, clothes, gold, silver, and jewels which they found with the enemy dead. For three days, they did not allow anyone to come to look for the bodies of the fallen nobles. However, on the third day, the Swiss made a truce with the Austrians and allowed many of their dead to be removed. By that time, the stench of the dead was awful because the weather was very

---

74 Twinger in Liebenau, *Sempach*, p.118.
75 Rupp in Liebenau, *Sempach*, p.173.
76 Dacher in Liebenau, *Sempach*, p.175.
77 Etterlin in Liebenau, *Sempach*, p.207.
78 Schodeler in Liebenau, *Sempach*, p.215.
79 Rudolf Henggeler, (ed.) *Das Schlachtenjahrzeit der Eidgenossen nach den innerschweizerischen Jahrzeitbüchern*. (Basel: Birkhäuser, 1940)
80 Tschudi in Liebenau, *Sempach*, pp.256–259.
81 Tschudi in Liebenau, *Sempach*, p.256.

hot, and the corpses had begun to decay. The families of the fallen nobles came with great anguish and sorrow to find the bodies of the Duke and the great lords, which numbered roughly 60 men. About 40 of them, including Leopold, were initially interred in the monastery at Königsfelden, and the others were carried away to their lands for burial. No one wanted to remove the remaining bodies because of their stench in the heat, so a big pit was dug on the battlefield, and the bodies were thrown into it. Later, a small chapel was built on that spot.[82] The chapel was later rebuilt and renovated several times, but it still stands on the location of the mass burial.

82 Twinger in Liebenau, *Sempach*, pp.118–119 and *Oesterreichische Chronik* in Liebenau, *Sempach*, p.114.

7

The Battle of Näfels, 9 April 1388

Background to Battle

Inspired by the victory at Sempach, the canton of Bern, which had been reluctant to get involved in the struggle, took the field and pressed its power into the nearby area of Fribourg. In addition, Bern expanded its holdings in the mountainous areas south of the canton now known as the Berner Oberland or Bernese Highlands. The Swiss Confederation also took advantage of the victory at Sempach to renew its ties with Glarus, which became more aggressive in weakening Habsburg influence in the area. Soon, with the help of the Swiss, the Glarners took control of the Austrian town of Weesen in August 1386. Weesen was at a strategic location on the west end of Lake Walensee near the location where the Linth River flows into the lake. The Glarus Canton rests in a deep, glacial valley carved out of the high foothills of the Alps, and its only convenient line of communication was down the Linth River Valley through Weesen. Therefore, whoever controlled the town at the mouth of the Linth dominated commerce going into and out of the canton, and the Glarners knew they had to take Weesen to command access to their homeland. The Glarners also established a garrison in the town and drove out the Austrian officials, which precipitated further action from the Habsburgs.

Duke Leopold's heir, William the Courteous or *Wilhelm der Freundliche* (the friendly) (ca. 1370–1406) was only about 16 years old at the time of his father's death at Sempach. This meant that Leopold's brother, Duke Albert III (1349–1395), served as regent, and it was up to him to avenge his brother's death and regain family prestige by retaking Weesen and Glarus. In the night of 21–22 February 1388, the loyal citizens of Weesen opened the gates of the walls around the town which allowed the Austrians to overwhelm the sleeping Swiss garrison there in what has been called the 'Night of Murder in Weesen' (*Mordnacht von Weesen*). The Habsburgs decided to follow up this victory with a full-scale invasion of Glarus, and they assembled an army of 5,000 or 6,000 men on horseback and on foot in the effort.[1] One source maintained that the force was 15,000 men, but this was a clear exaggeration.[2] Faced with the threat of a large belligerent force on their borders, the people of Glarus desperately tried to negotiate a peace, and they hoped to receive mercy from the Austrians, even though they no longer trusted the nobles. These efforts failed, and military action soon followed.[3]

The leaders of the Habsburg forces were Count Johann I von Werdenberg-Sargans (1342/3–1400), Peter von Torberg, and Johanns von Klingenberg as well as other lords, knights, and squires. The nobles were accompanied by forces from 'Schaffhausen, Winterthur, Frauenfeld, Radolfzell, Rapperswil, and others.'[4] In an historical irony, which is similar to the situation when Zurich supported the enemies of Schwyz at the Battle of Morgarten, all of these cities' best interest in the long run rested with their defeat and the victory of Glarus which they were attacking. Each one of these areas, with the exception of Radolfzell, would later join the Swiss Confederation as valued members.

Austrian troops plundering Näfels in 1388. Diebold Schilling the Younger, *Eidgenössische Chronik des Luzerners*, Lucerne, 1513. (ZHB Luzern Sondersammlung, S 23 fol.)

The Austrian Advance

On 9 April 1388, the entire Austrian army 'with all its power and might' advanced on Glarus. The Glarners had been concerned about such an attack after the nobles had taken Weesen, and sentinels had been placed to watch for any enemy movements night and day. When these troops saw the approach of the enemy forces, they immediately sounded the alarm to the men of Glarus calling them to assemble. They also sent messengers over the Pragel Pass to Schwyz and over the Klausen Pass to Uri urgently requesting aid as soon as possible. The Glarners were convinced that they needed to meet the threat as promptly to prevent a full-scale conquest of their territory, so they decided to rush their forces to the border defences to make a stand even against long odds.[5]

1 *Klingenberger Chronik*, p.132.
2 *Chronik der Stadt Zürich*, p.141.
3 *Klingenberger Chronik*, p.132.
4 *Chronik der Stadt Zürich*, pp.137–139.
5 Frey, *Kriegstaten der Schweizer*, p.117.

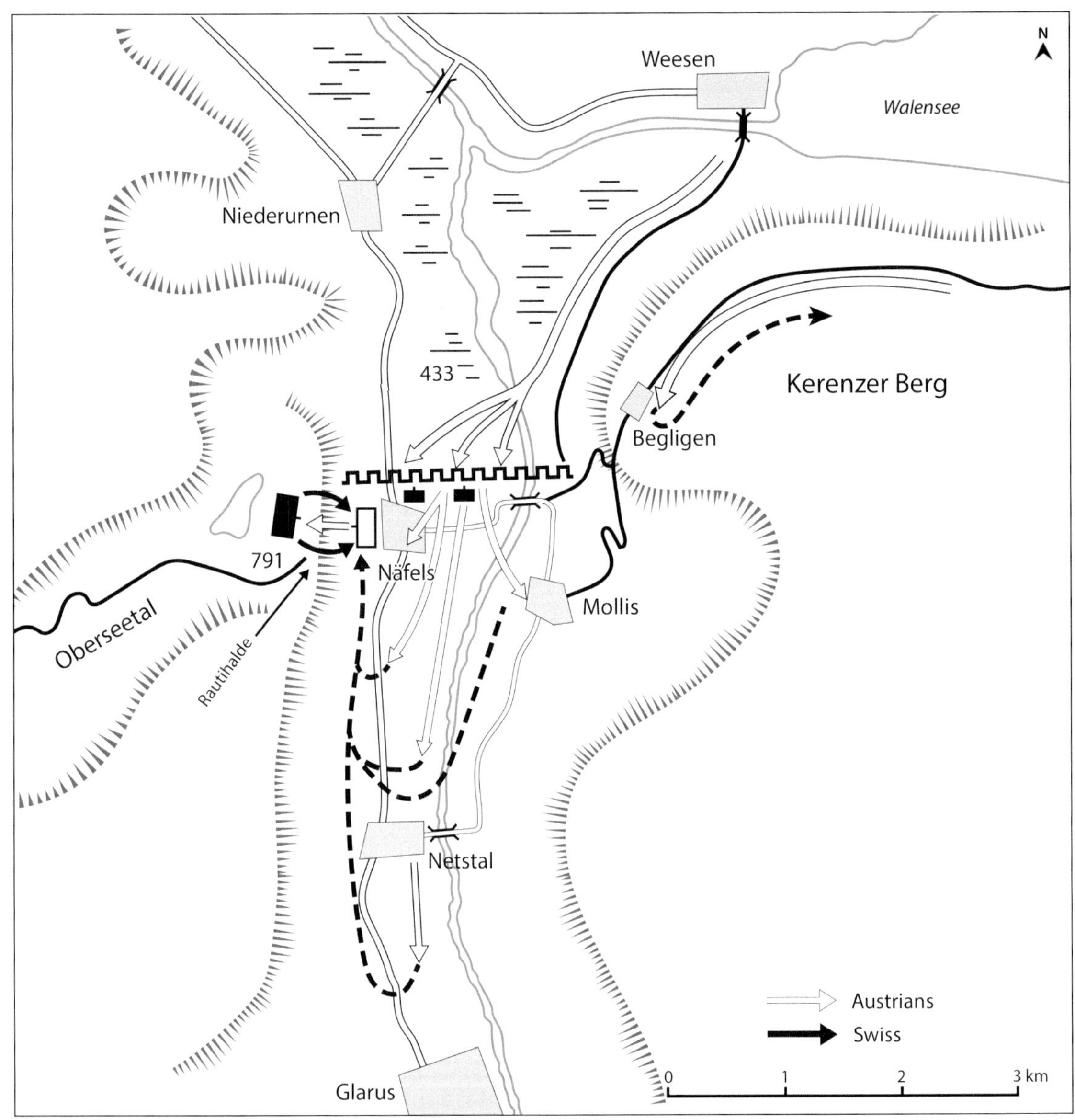

The Battle of Näfels, 9 April 1388

Schwyz and Uri seemed to react as rapidly as possible, but the distance over the high mountain passes prevented them from sending large numbers of men in a timely manner. Only a meagre contingent of 50 men from Schwyz was believed to have arrived in time to participate in the battle, and a smaller number of men from Uri was present as well. Presumably, the bells of church towers rang up the valley of Glarus, and the men assembled as rapidly as possible. The total number of men from Glarus was reported as 350, but their entire force might have been 400 after adding the men from Schwyz. Yet this calculation might be too modest, because at least one modern historian has argued that the manpower potential of Glarus might have been 500 or 600 men.[6] If the larger number of 500 to 600 men from Glarus was correct, and if the statement that 5,000 to 6,000 Austrians was also accurate, then the Glarners and their allies were outnumbered by a factor of at least 10 to one.

Glarus Controls the Battle

The Glarners and their allies assembled their forces on a mountain top near the village of Näfels. Apparently, there was insufficient time to place their entire force behind the border defences (*Letzi*), so there was a smaller contingent on hand to meet the threat of invasion at that location, which protected the entrance into the long valley that formed Glarus. These *Letzi* or border defences were largely a wall running roughly 1,500 metres (about 1,640 yards) from the base of the Rautispitz Mountain northward all the way to the slopes of the Beglingen. The exact dimensions of the defences are unclear, but they were perhaps a metre and a half high (five feet) and about a metre wide (three feet). In addition, there was a three-metre wide trench (10 feet) on the outside of the wall facing the direction of any potential enemy threat. No doubt, this impressive defensive line took many years and great expense to construct, but its effectiveness in protecting the area proved to be only limited. The *Letzi* could clearly break up a cavalry attack, but these defences could be expected to accomplish little more against a foe who greatly outnumbered the Glarners.[7]

Yet taking a stand behind these border defences made good sense, because these positions helped the Glarners meet their adversaries at less of a disadvantage, but all they could expect to accomplish was to buy time. The men of Glarus and their allies tried to hold the position, but the Austrians overran the defences early in the day and 'killed many [men] at the *Letzi*' who had stubbornly tried to stand against the attack. The Glarners and their allies fell back in disorder, but they soon rallied and took up a position on a nearby mountain. Many in the Austrian army believed they had won the

6 *Chronik der Stadt Zürich*, p.140. Footnote by Johannes Dierauer.
7 Frey, *Kriegstaten der Schweizer*, p.117.

battle and failed to press their advantage to pursue and destroy the fleeing enemy. The Habsburg troops marched deep into Glarus where they burned houses, laid waste to the area, and plundered anything of value. They rounded up and captured over 1,200 heads of cattle, which they planned to drive away because they thought no one would oppose them.[8]

While the plundering continued, some of the nobles finally paid attention to the men from Glarus who had assembled on the mountain, and the knights rode against them. This advance was poorly planned because it gave up many of the advantages the cavalrymen enjoyed. They would not be able to charge their adversaries because of the steep incline, and they would have difficulty in keeping good order while advancing up the slope. Additionally, many men in the Austrian army had scattered to pillage and plunder meaning that their numerical advantage over the men from Glarus had been greatly diminished at the point of contact. The Glarners and their allies took advantage of the inherent weaknesses in the knights' advance and staged a counterattack that was perfectly timed. They first threw stones down the slope onto the cavalry which caused the enemy horses to become frightened and unmanageable. The nobles called to the men advancing behind them to pull back, so the stones thrown by their enemies would not kill them. When these men retreated, the Glarners took advantage of the moment and struck with all their men who were wielding halberds and other pole arms. The Austrians were pushed back in confusion, and their position rapidly became untenable. The knights were unable to withstand the attack, and they soon panicked and fled.[9]

The Battle of Näfels, 9 April 1388. Diebold Schilling the Younger, *Eidgenössische Chronik des Luzerners*, Lucerne, 1513. (ZHB Luzern Sondersammlung, S 23 fol.)

The men from Glarus pressed their advance over a great swamp all the way to Weesen and killed 400 or 500 men before they reached the bridge that either went over the Wag stream or the Linth River.[10] Some of the Austrians were in such a state of confusion and fear that they offered little or no resistance before they were killed. Others tried to rally and defend themselves in small groups, but they were cut down as well because the Glarners had these small bunches of men outnumbered at the point of contact. In desperation to flee and survive, the Austrians rushed heavily to the bridge over the Wag or the Linth. The pressure to cross was so strong, and the troops weighed so much that the structure collapsed throwing numerous men into the water where many of them drowned. These men were in such hysteria in the water that none of them paid attention to others, and they pushed each other down in an attempt to escape, but their

8 *Klingenberger Chronik*, p.132.
9 *Klingenberger Chronik*, pp.132–133.
10 *Klingenberger Chronik*, p.133.

heavy arms and armour made getting away all the more challenging. The earliest sources stated that the number of men who drowned in this manner was unknown, but there were many of them.[11]

There were still quite a few nobles in the area who had apparently been sent on a flanking manoeuvre to attack the border defences of Glarus in case the main frontal attack on the *Letzi* failed. Count Johann von Sargans was leading this contingent of 1,500 men, which advanced over the Beglingen hillside at a critical moment. From that position, he could see how the battle was progressing, with the Glarners, apparently in some disorder, pursuing the Austrians. There may have been an opportunity to attack the men from Glarus at a distinct advantage at that point, but Sargans refused to engage the enemy. Rather, he turned, led his men off the field, and fell back to Weesen. This was the last opportunity the Austrians had of changing the outcome of the battle, and it had been missed.

The Glarners and their allies pursued their enemies all the way to Weesen before they returned to the battlefield and 'beat to death all those who were not yet dead.' In other words, they killed all the wounded Austrians rather than take them captive. The victorious soldiers then took all the armour and clothing off the dead men all the way to their undergarments. They then buried the bodies together in three mass graves in the meadow in front of the *Letzi* where the Habsburg forces had overwhelmed the Glarners earlier in the battle.[12] The surviving Austrians fled to Weesen, but they soon decided to withdraw. On 11 April 1388, two days after the battle, the Austrians burned Weesen, and they took the women and children with them and left.[13]

The Cost of the Battle

So unexpected and complete was the victory that an Austrian source suggested that the Glarners had cast a spell on their enemies causing a fog and darkness to appear on the battlefield, which prevented the Habsburg army from seeing its opponents.[14] All myths aside, the triumph was truly remarkable. It was achieved against the longest odds of any major victory in Swiss history. The Austrian losses in the battle were severe. A list of the prominent Habsburg dead included 55 names, and the total number of Austrian dead was usually placed between 400 and 500 before the fleeing army reached the bridge, but the total losses were much higher.[15] Two additional early sources stated that the Habsburg total loss was 2,400 killed.

11 *Klingenberger Chronik*, p.133.
12 *Klingenberger Chronik*, p.133.
13 *Klingenberger Chronik*, pp.131–137, Justinger, *Die Berner-Chronik,* p.169, and *Chronik der Stadt Zürich*, pp.137–140.
14 Dacher's *Konstanzerchronik* as cited in *Klingenberger Chronik*, p.135.
15 *Klingenberger Chronik*, pp.133–134.

'And the enemy dead who remained [on the battlefield] were more than 2,400 men.' The Glarners also captured 13 flags and took much armour.[16] One source broke down the numbers more succinctly. In this case, 1,800 Austrians were killed on the battlefield, and the remainder drowned in the Linth River and in Lake Walensee near Weesen.[17] The bodies had been buried in three mass a graves in front of the border defences regardless of their rank, but many were later exhumed and reinterred elsewhere. Some 20 months after the battle the abbot, Bilgeri von Rüti, came to the location and found 180 bodies, which he removed to be interred at the monastery of Rüti in the modern Zurich Canton. Despite the obvious stench of rotting corpses, the abbot insisted on having everybody he could find exhumed and properly buried.[18]

The Battle of Näfels, 9 April 1388. Diebold Schilling the Younger, *Eidgenössische Chronik des Luzerners*, Lucerne, 1513 (ZHB Luzern Sondersammlung, S 23 fol.)

In comparison, the casualties suffered by Glarus were light, and only 54 Glarners were killed. A book of yearly commemoration broke down the numbers a bit further, and it stated that 51 Glarners died in the battle as well as two from Uri and one from Schwyz.[19] Presumably, all these men were properly buried in the parish church at Mollis in the Glarus Canton.

The Swiss Win their Independence

After the Battle of Näfels, the war continued inconclusively. A coalition of forces from Zurich, Lucerne, Uri, Schwyz, Unterwalden, and Bern laid siege to Rapperswil on the other side of Lake Zurich from the city of Zurich. These forces attempted to storm the town on 1 May 1388, and they managed to take one house within the city walls, but a garrison of more than 700 able combatants retook the structure. They then forced the Swiss to retreat with a loss of 40 men dead. After this failure, the various besieging forces disbanded and went home.[20]

Yet the Swiss soon staged other attacks, and after they destroyed a number of enemy castles, both sides of the conflict were nearing exhaustion. Finally, in April 1389 the imperial cities negotiated an armistice for seven years. During that time, the Habsburgs tried to gain an advantage over members

16 Justinger, *Die Berner-Chronik*, p.170.
17 *Chronik der Stadt Zürich*, p.140 and Justinger, *Die Berner-Chronik*, p.170.
18 *Klingenberger Chronik*, pp.136–137.
19 *Chronik der Stadt Zürich*, pp.140–141 in Dierauer's footnote.
20 Justinger, *Die Berner-Chronik*, p.170.

of the Confederation by attempting to undermine some of the Swiss Cantons politically, but this effort proved to be counterproductive, and the Austrians seemed to make more enemies than friends. On 16 July 1394, the truce of seven years was extended to 20 years. In May 1412, another treaty was signed extending the peace for yet another 50 years. These series of agreements essentially ended the war the Swiss had fought to end Habsburg domination in their lands for nearly a century. Through military action, the Swiss had in effect finally won their independence.

If the Swiss had failed, the consequences might have been severe. At exactly the same time as the members of the Swiss Confederation were creating democracies and defending their privileges as free men, other similar efforts failed. For example, the Jacquerie Peasants' Revolt in France in 1358, the Peasants' Revolt in England in 1381, and the Ciompi Revolt in Florence from 1378 to 1382 all ended in failure, and the rights of the lower classes remained restricted. On 23 August 1388, less than five months after the Battle of Näfels, a coalition of noble factions defeated the forces of the Swabian City League (*Schwäbische Städtebund*) of southern Germany at the Battle of Döffingen. This led to the dissolution of the City League in the next year, which ended any hope that these cities could create a coalition similar to the Swiss to protect their independence.[21] Clearly, the Swiss military successes spelled the difference between their ability to look after their own affairs or to be controlled by noble factions that were often hostile to their interests.

21 Dändliker, *Geschichte der Schweiz*, vol. 1, p.605.

8

The Sempach Letter of 1393 and the Laws of War

In the late fourteenth century, the Swiss Confederation was strengthening its ties to each other by the creation of its earliest system of laws held in common by all its members. The cantons were no longer willing to suffer the inconsistencies of the different states administering varying policies on matters of common concern, and the members decided to create a body of rules ostensibly binding on each. The first charter defining such concord was the Priests' Charter (*Pfaffenbrief*) of 7 October 1370, which was signed by six members of the Eight Old Cantons including Zurich, Lucerne, Zug, Uri, Schwyz, and Unterwalden. Bern and Glarus were not represented. One of the charter's principal concerns was to assure that foreign clergymen would not act independently of Swiss laws and interests by professing citizenship elsewhere, thus assuring that these clerics would be subject to the secular courts of the Confederation. There were also several clauses in the Charter dealing with the regulation of traffic flowing along the routes from the St. Gotthard Pass to Zurich. Additionally, the document was designed to help keep the peace, and there were also injunctions forbidding civil war. The appropriate police powers were also proscribed to keep the peace.[1]

The next step in providing unified rules among the Swiss Cantons was the highly significant Sempach Letter (*Sempacherbrief*) of 10 July 1393. This was an attempt to regulate the conduct of Swiss troops in campaigns and in battle. The cantons were not only expanding the nature of their military alliance, but the agreement also proved to be a landmark policy in the development of the laws of war. The conduct of men in battle and on campaigns had long been directed by custom, the moral admonitions of the Church, and the vague ideas of chivalry, but very little had been codified into a standard set of rules. The signatories of the Sempach letter were the Eight Old Cantons, including Uri, Schwyz, Unterwalden, Lucerne,

1 Oechsli, *Quellenbuch*, pp.110–113 and *Eidgenössische Abschiede*, 1, pp.301–303.

Zug, Zurich, Bern, and Glarus. Significantly, Solothurn also agreed to the concord. Even though it was long friendly to the Confederation, Solothurn only became a full member of the alliance in 1481.

The provisions of the Sempach Letter included a prohibition of plundering until the conclusion of battle and then only with the permission of the leaders. Also included were rules for the distribution of booty, a charge strictly forbidding the Swiss to fight among themselves, a rule stating that all offenders of military laws be tried by the testimony of two witnesses, a charge that the Swiss wounded should be tended, and a strict admonition that no one should flee from battle. The charter gave special protection to Churches, women, and children, but no such allowance was made for men.[2]

The significance of the letter was far-reaching. The Swiss would take further steps later to regulate military action, but the Sempach Letter had a considerable impact on the further development of such rules. The enforcement of these provisions was left up to the individual cantons of the Confederation or to the actual leaders in the field as the possible circumstances arose, but there were then recognised rules to form the guidelines for military conduct. The Sempach Letter would influence the military laws of Bern in 1410, as amended in 1415, as well as the military rules of Bern in 1443, as amended in 1448. In a similar manner, the Sempach Letter had an influence on the Zurich military rules of 1444 and on the Confederation's military statutes of 1476 and again in 1499.[3]

2 *Eidgenössische Abschiede*, 1, pp.327–379 and Oechsli, *Quellenbuch*, pp.125–127.

3 Berner *Kriegsordnung* 26 May 1410 and 28 March 1415; and 11 August 1443 and 2 January 1448 in Eugen von Frauenholz. *Das Heerwesen der Schweizer Eidgenossenschaft* (München: Beck, 1936), pp.130–134 and *Zürcher Kriegsordnung* 10 May 1444 in Frauenholz, *Heerwesen*, pp.134–136. See also, Gotts. Friedr. Ochsenbein, *Die Kriegsgründe und Kreigsbilder des Burgunderkriegs* (Bern: Jent & Reinert, 1876), pp.46–48 and *Eidgenössische Abschiede* 3, p.600.

9

Conclusion: The Swiss Military System in Development

The fourteenth century was a highly significant time in the formation and preservation of the Swiss Confederation against the various threats from noble factions, most importantly from the Habsburg family. While the frequent warfare of the era often involved raids and sieges, four major battles took place that went far to decide the outcome of various wars. The Battles of Morgarten, Laupen, Sempach, and Näfels virtually assured the survival and independence of the Swiss Cantons, and they did much to develop the Swiss military system. These successes were not only important for Swiss history and the creation of a coalition that eventually became modern Switzerland. But these victories were more important than only to help create a political entity, because these successes also allowed a free people to retain their privileges and liberties.

Yet the Swiss military was still in its early formation in the fourteenth century, and much needed developments had to follow for the cantons to be successful in maintaining their independence and extending their power. The next half century, roughly from 1400 to 1450, would witness the improvement of the Swiss as an effective early infantry, most notably in the Battles of Voegelinsegg (1403), Stoss (1405), Arbedo (1422), and St. Jakob an der Birs (1444). These important contests took place mostly during the Appenzell Wars (1403–1428) and the Zurich War (1436–1450). The famous Swiss pike squares were developed in this era that were highly disciplined and capable of complex manoeuvres in both the offense and defence. The Swiss also became an important model in the advancement of effective tactical infantries in many places of Europe at that time.

Bibliography

Primary Sources

Anonymous, *Amtliche Sammlung der ältern Eidgenössische Abschiede,* 8 vols. (Luzern: Wener'sche Buchdruckerei, 1861–1874)

Anonymous, 'Klagerodel: 1311, nach März 14 Juni 19,' *Der Geschichtsfreund: Mitteilungen des Historischen Vereins der fünf Orte Luzern, Uri, Schwyz, Underwalden Ob und Nid dem Wald und Zug* 43(1888), pp.345–359

Anonymous, *Fontes Rerum Bernensium: Bern's Geschichtsquellen,* 10 vols. (Bern: K. Schmidt, 1887–1956)

Bernoulli, August (ed.), *Basler Chroniken,* 7 vols. (Leipzig: S. Hirzel, 1872–1915)

Brennwald, Heinrich, *Schweizerchronik,* 2 vols. (Basel: Basler Buch und Antiquariatshandlung, 1910)

Bruckner, A. and B. (eds.), *Schweizer Fahnenbuch* (St. Gallen: Zollikofer, 1942)

Dierauer, Johannes (ed.), *Chronik der Stadt Zürich* (Basel: Adolf Geering, 1900)

Escher, J. and Schweizer P., (eds.) *Urkundenbuch der Stadt und Landschaft Zürich,* 13 vols. (Zürich: Höhr, 1888–[1957])

Etterlin, Petermann, *Kronica von der loblichen Eidgnossenschaft* (Basel: Daniel Eckenstein, 1752)

Fründ, Hans, (Christian Immanuel Kind, ed.) *Die Chronik des Hans Fründ, Landschreiber zu Schwytz* (Chur: Gengel, 1875)

Grieshaber, Karl, (ed.) *Oberrheinische Chronik*: Älteste bis jetzt bekannte in Deutscher Prosa (Rastatt: Publisher unknown, 1850)

Henggeler, Rudolf, (ed.) *Das Schlachtenjahrzeit der Eidgenossen nach den innerschweizerischen Jahrzeitbüchern* (Basel: Birkhäuser, 1940)

Huber, August, (ed.) *Urkundenbuch der Stadt Basel*, 6 vols. (Basel: R. Reich, 1899–1902)

Justinger, Conrad, (G. Studer, ed.) *Die Berner-Chronik, nebst vier Beilagen:* 1) *Cronica de Berno.* 2) *Conflictus Laupensis.* 3) *Die anonyme Stadtchronik* oder *der Königshofen-Justinger.* 4) *Anonymus Freiburgensis* (Bern: K. J. Wyss, 1871)

Kopp, J.E. (ed.) *Urkunden zur Geschichte der eidgenössischen Bünde* (Luzern: Meyer, 1835)

Liebenau, Theodor von (ed.), 'Berichte über die Schlacht am Morgarten,' *Mitteilungen des Historischen Vereins des Kantons Schwyz* 3 (1884) [Includes 93 early sources]

Liebenau, Theodor von (ed.) *Die Schlacht bei Sempach Gedenkbuch zur fünften Säcularfeier* (Luzern: C.F. Prell, 1886). [Includes 204 reports, which includes many histories and chronicles; 70 yearly death commemorations and obituaries; 20 songs and sayings; 27 documents, council decisions, and bills; [13] reports of trophies and relics; [142] descriptions of pictures; 13 descriptions of monuments; 9 descriptions of commemorative medals; 23 folk tales; and 4 descriptions of celebrations of battle commemorations]

Neuenburg, Mathias von, (Adolf Hofmeister, ed.) *Die Chronik des Mathias von Neuenburg,* (Berlin: Weidmann, 1955)

Oechsli, W. (ed.), *Die Anfänge der Schweizerischen Eidgenossenschaft: zur sechsten Säkularfeier des ersten ewigen Bundes vom 1. August 1291* (Zürich: Ulrich & Co., 1891). [Includes many primary sources in the appendix]

Oechsli, Wilhelm (ed.), *Quellenbuch zur Schweizergeschichte*: *Neue Folge* (ed.) and *kleine Ausgabe* (ed.) (Zürich: Schulthess, 1893 and 1918)

Russ, Melchior, (August Bernoulli, ed.) *Die Luzernerchronik* (Basel: Schultze, 1872)

Sargans, Anton Henne von, (ed.) *Klingenberger Chronik* (Gotha: Parthes, 1861)

Sieber, Ludwig, 'Zwei neue Berichte über das Erdbeben von 1356,' *Beiträge zur vertländischen Geschichte. Neue Folge* 2 (1888) pp.113–124

Thommen, Rudolf (ed.) *Urkunden zur Schweizer Geschichte aus Österreichischen Archiven,* 4 vols. (Basel: Geering, 1900)

Winterthur, Johannes von, (Georg von Wyss ed.) *Johannis Vitodurani Chronicon: Die Chronik des Minoriten Johannes von Winterthur* (Zürich: Höhr, 1856)

Secondary Sources

Amgwerd, Carl, 'Die Schlacht und das Schlachtfeld von Morgarten,' *Mitteilungen des Historischen Vereins des Kantons Schwyz* 49 (1951), pp.1–[221]

Anonymous, *Arnold von Winkelried: Mythos und Wirklichkeit* (Stans: Historischer Verein Nidwalden, 1986)

Bernoulli, August, *Winkelrieds That bei Sempach: eine kritische Untersuchung* (Basel: C. Detloff, 1886)

Boeheim, Wendelin, *Handbuch der Waffenkunde in seiner historischen Entwickelung von Beginn des Mittelalters bis zum Ende des 18. Jahrhunderts* (Leipzig: Seeman, 1890)

Bresslau, H[arry] 'Das älteste Bündnis der Schweizer Urkantone,' *Jahrbuch für schweizerische Geschichte* 20 (1895), pp.29–32

Bürgi, Jost, 'Die Letzinen der Urkantone: ein Verteidigungssystem aus der Zeit der Bundesgründung,' *Mitteilungen des Historischen Vereins des Kantons Schwyz* 75 (1983), pp.27–56

Bürkli, Karl, *Der wahre Winkelried: die Taktik der alten Urschweizer* (Zürich: Schabelitz, 1886)

Castell, Anton, *Die Bundesbriefe zu Schwyz: Volkstümliche Darstellung wichtiger Urkunden Eidgenössischer Frühzeit* (Einsiedeln: Benziger, 1969)

Dändliker, Karl, *Geschichte der Schweiz: mit besonderer Rücksicht auf die Entwicklung des Verfassungs- und Kulturlebens von den ältesten Zeiten bis zur Gegenwart*, 3 vols. (Zürich: Friedrich Schulthess, 1900)

Delbrück, Hans, *Geschichte der Kriegskunst im Rahmen der politischen Geschichte*, 6 vols., vol. 3: *das Mittelalter* (Berlin: Stilke, 1923)

Delbrück, Hans, (Walter J. Renfroe, Jr. trans.) *History of the Art of War*, vol. 3 *medieval Warfare* (Lincoln: University of Nebraska Press, 1990)

DeVries, Kelly, *Infantry Warfare: in the early Fourteenth Century: Discipline, Tactics, and Technology* (Rochester, NY: Boydell, 1998)

Dierauer, Johannes, *Geschichte der schweizerischen Eidgenossenschaft*, 5 vols. (Gotha: Perthes, 1887–1917)

Dürr, Emil. 'Die Politik der Eidgenossen im XIV und XV Jahrhundert,' *Schweizer Kriegsgeschichte* 4 (1933), pp.460–503

Elgger, Carl von, *Kriegswesen und Kriegskunst der Schweizerischen Eidgenossen im XIV., XV. und XVI. Jahrhundert* (Lucerne: Militärisches Verlagsbureau, 1873)

Feller, Richard and Edgar Bonjour, *Geschichtschreibung der Schweiz: vom Spätmittelalter zur Neuzeit* (Basel: Helbing & Lichtenhahn, 1979)

Frauenholz, Eugen von. *Das Heerwesen der Schweizer Eidgenossenschaft* (München: Beck, 1936)

Frey, Emil, *Kriegstaten der Schweizer: dem Volk erzählt* (Neuenburg: Bahn, [1904])

Geiser, Karl, 'Die Verfassung des alten Bern.' *Festschrift zur VII. Säkularfeier der Gründung Berns 1191–1891* 4 (Bern, 1891), pp.1–141

Gessler, Edward A., *Das Schweizerische Geschützwesen zur Zeit des Schwabenkriegs, 1499* (Zürich: Kommissionsverlag, 1927)

Gessler, Edward A., 'Die Waffenübungen der Jungend in der alten Eidgenossenschaft mit besoderer Berücksichtigung Zürichs,' *Zürich Taschenbuch* 23 (1923), pp.195–220

Gleser, Johann Heinrich, *Specimen observationum ex iure gentium et iure publico circa Helvetiorum foedera* (Basilaeae: Rudolfum Im-Hof, 1760)

Hadron, Walter, 'Neues zur Laupenschlacht,' *Blätter für Bernischen Geschichte, Kunst, und Altertumskunde* 3 (May 1907), pp.120–125

Häne, Johannes, 'Die Kriegsbereitschaft der alten Eidgnossen,' *Schweizer Kriegsgeschichte* 3 (1915), pp.5–33

Hartmann, Otto, *Die Schlacht bei Sempach: historisch-kritische Studie* (Frauenfeld: Huber, 1886)

Helfenstein, Fanny, *Die Schlacht bei Sempach: eine Analyse von Mythos, Realität und ihrer Bedeutung für die Schweizer Identität* (Hamburg: Tradition, 2024)

Hobohm, Martin, *Machiavellis Renaissance der Kriegskunst* (Berlin: Karl Curtius, 1913)

Hohlenstein, Walther ab, *Urschweizer Bundesbrief 1291: Untersuchungen zur Immanenten Bestimmung seines Zeugnisses* (St. Gallen: Schloss Schwarzenbach, 1956)

Hübscher, Bruno. *Die Entwicklung und Struktur des Luzernischen Heerwesens von 1291–1500.* (Hochdorf: Buchdrückerei Hochdorf, 1943)

Hug, Lina and Richard Stead, *Switzerland* (New York, NY: Putnam's Sons, 1920)

Kern, Léon, 'Notes: pour servir à un débat sur le pacte de 1291,' *Zeitschrift für schweizerische Geschichte*, 9 (1929), pp.340–346

Kurz, Hans Rudolf, *Schweizerschlachten* (Bern: Francke, 1962)

Laffont, Robert, *The Ancient Art of Warfare,* 2 vols. (Paris: Robert Laffont, 1966)

Lang, Beatrix. *Der Guglerkrieg: ein Kapitel Dynastengeschichte im Vorfeld des Sempacherkrieges* (Fribourg: Universitätsverlag Freiburg, 1982)

Largiadèr, Anton, *Geschichte von Stadt und Landschaft Zürich* (Zürich: Rentsch, 1945)

Liebenau, Hermann von, *Lebens-Geschichte der Königin Agnes von Ungarn: der letzten Habsburgerin des erlauchten Stammhauses as dem Aargaue* (Regensburg: Georg Joseph Manz, 1868)

Marchal, Guy P., *Sempach 1386: von den Anfängen des Territorialstaates Luzern; Beitrag zur Frühgeschichte des Kantons Luzern* (Basel, Helbing und Lichtenhahn, 1986)

Meyer, Bruno, *Die Ältesten Eidgenössischen Bünde: Neue Untersuchungen über die Anfänge der Schweizerischen Eidgenossenschaft* (Zürich: Rentsch, 1938)

Meyer, Bruno, 'Die Entstehung der Eidgenossenschaft: Der Stand der heutigen Anschauungen,' *Schweizerische Zeitschrift für Geschichte* 2 (1952), pp.153–205

Meyer, Bruno, 'Die Schlacht am Morgarten: Verlauf der Schlacht und Absichten der Parteien,' *Schweizerische Zeitschrift für Geschichte* 16: 2 (1966), pp.129–179

Meyer, Karl, 'Der Ursprung der Eidgenossenschaft,' *Zeitschrift für schweizerische Geschichte* 21: 3 (1941), pp.285–652

Moser, Franz, 'Der Laupenkrieg, 1339' in *Archiv des Historischen Vereins des Kantons Bern* 35: 1 (1939), pp.1–174

Müller, Johannes von, *Sämmtliche Werke*, 27 vols. (Tübingen: J.G. Cotta'schen Buchhandlung, 1810–1819)

Müller, Philipp, 'Morgarten: ein Beitrag zur Waffentechnik,' *Mitteilungen des Historischen Vereins des Kantons Schwyz* 88 (1996), pp.23–40.

Niederstätter, Alois, *Die Herrschaft Österreich: Fürst und Land im Spätmittelalter* (Wien: Ueberreuter, 2001)

Nüscheler, A., 'Die Letzinen in der Schweiz,' *Mittheilungen der*

Antiquarischen Gesellschaft in Zürich 18 (1872), pp.1–62

Ochsenbein, Gotts. Friedr. *Die Kriegsgründe und Kriegsbilder des Burgunderkriegs* (Bern: Jent & Reinert, 1876)

Oman, Charles, *A History of the Art of War in the Middle Ages*, vol. 2, *1278–1485* (New York: Franklin, 1924)

Padrutt, Christian, *Staat und Krieg im alten Bünden* (Zürich: Fretz und Wasmuth, 1965)

Pfister, Christoph, *Bern und die alten Eidgenossen: Die Entstehung der Schwyzer Eidgenossenschaft im Lichte der Geschichtskritick*, (Norderstedt: Dillum, 2006)

Pfister, Christoph, 'Der Bundesbrief von 1291: Kritik einer Gefälschten Urkunde,' www.dillum.dh/html/bundesbrief_1291_kritik.htm

Riggenbach, Andreas, *Der Marchenstreit zwischen Schwyz und Einsiedeln und die Entstehung der Eidgenossenschaft* (Zürich: Fretz und Wasmuth, 1965)

Sablonier, Rogert, '1315–ein weiteres Gründungsjahr der Eidgenossenschaft? Der Bundesbrief von 1315' *Der Geschichtsfreund: Mitteilungen des historischen Vereins Zentralschweiz* 160 (2007), pp.9–24

Sablonier, Roger, *Gründungszeit ohne Eidgenossen: Politik und Gesellschaft in der Innerschweiz um 1300* (Baden: hier + jetzt, 2008)

Sablonier, Roger, 'Schweizer Eidgenossenschaft im 15. Jahrhundert: Staatlichkeit, Politik und Selbstverständnis,' in *Die Entstehung der Schweiz: vom Bundesbrief 1291 zur*

Nationalen Geschichtskultur des 20. Jahrhunderts (Schwyz: Historischer Verein des Kantons Schwyz, 1999), pp.9–42

Schaufelberger,Walter, *Die alte Schweizer und sein Kreig: Studien zur Kriegführung vornehmlich in 15. Jahrhundert* (Zürich: Europa, 1952)

Schneider, Hugo, 'Die Bewaffnung zur Zeit der Schlacht am Morgarten,' *Mitteilungen des Historischen Vereins des Kantons Schwyz* 58 (1965) pp.37–49

Schneider, Hugo, 'Schwert und Dolch aus der Zeit der Schlacht am Morgarten, 1315,' *Mitteilungern des Historischen Vereins des Kantons Schwyz* 57 (1964) pp.137–46

Schweizer, Alexander, *Eine Studie zur Schlacht bei Sempach 9. Juli 1386* (Zürich: Berichthaus, 1902)

Schweizer, Paul, 'Die Freiheit der Schwyzer,' *Jahrbuch für Schweizerische Geschichte* 10 (1885), pp.2–25

Sidler, Wilhelm, *Die Schlacht am Morgarten* (Zürich: Orell Füßli, 1910)

Sieber, Marc, 'Johann Heinrich Gleser (1734–1773) und die Wiederentdeckung des Bundesbriefs von 1291,' *Basler Zeitschrift für Geschichte und Altertumskunde* 91 (1991), pp.107–128

Sonderegger, Stefan, 'Der Kampf an der Letzi: Zur Typologie des spätmittelalterlichen Abwehrkampfes im Bereich von voralpinen Landwehren,' *Revue internationale d'histoire militaire* 65 (1988), pp.77–78

Stoessel, Everth, *Die Schlacht bei Sempach* (Berlin: Schulze, 1905)

Stürler, M. v. (Moritz von), *Der Laupenkrieg, 1339 und 1340; kritische beleuchtung der tradition als beitrag zur läuterung der ältern bernergeschichte* (Bern, Stämpfli'sche buchdruckerei, 1890)

Tuchman, Barbara W. *A Distant Mirror: the Calamitous 14th Century* (New York: Alfred A. Knopf, 1978)

Vincent, John Martin, *Switzerland at the Beginning of the Sixteenth Century* (Baltimore: Johns Hopkins Press, 1904)

Wattenwyl von Diesbach, Eduard von, *Geschichte der Stadt und Landschaft Bern: Dreizehntes Jahrhundert* (Schaffhausen: Hurter, 1867)

Wiget, Josef, (ed.) *Die Entstehung der Schweiz: von Bundesbrief 1291 zur Nationalen Geschichtskultur des 20. Jahrhunderts* (Schwyz: Satz, Druck und Repros, 1999)

Winkler, Albert, 'The Battle of Morgarten: an Essential Incident in the Founding of the Swiss State,' *Swiss American Historical Society Review*, 44: 3 (Nov. 2008), pp.3–25

Winkler, Albert, *The Swabian War of 1499: The first Confrontation between Landsknechts and the Swiss* (Warwick: Helion & Company, 2024)

Wirz, Hans Georg, *Zwischen Morgarten und Sempach: Laupen als Ring in der Kette* (Bern, A. Francke, [1935])

Wyß, Friedrich von, 'Die Freien Bauern, Freiämter, Freigerichte und die Vogteien der Ostschweiz im späteren Mittelalter,' *Zeitschrift für schweizerisches Recht* 18 (1873), pp.19–184

About the author

Albert Winkler has three masters' degrees and a Ph.D. in medieval Warfare, and his dissertation dealt with the Swiss military in the Middle Ages. He has published nearly sixty books and articles almost all dealing with military history, and he has been given two prestigious awards for the best article of the year in the Utah Historical Quarterly. He is currently a history instructor at Utah Valley University, and over six hundred students at that institution voted him teacher of the year in 2010.

About the artist

Giorgio Albertini is an Italian archaeologist, illustrator, and essayist celebrated for combining scientific accuracy with compelling visual storytelling. With a background in Medieval History, he has contributed to numerous excavation projects and published several scholarly essays on ancient and medieval warfare, daily life, and iconography. His detailed illustrations bring antiquity to life across books, museum exhibits, and academic journals. Collaborating with museums, publishers, and universities, Albertini bridges the gap between research and public engagement, making history accessible and vivid through both image and narrative.

A Time of Knights 400 CE to 1453 CE

The Battle of Adrianople (378 CE) marked the dominance of heavy cavalry over infantry, signalling the decline of the Western Roman Empire and the rise of feudalism. Nobles, in exchange for land, provided knights who became Europe's primary military force, clad in increasingly advanced armour. Beyond Europe, the Mongols relied on disciplined light cavalry, while the Islamic Caliphates combined light and heavy cavalry with trained infantry. China pioneered gunpowder weapons.

Castles and fortified cities shaped siege warfare, leading to increased use of artillery. By the late medieval period, longbows, pikes, and firearms challenged knights' battlefield dominance, ushering in military innovations that paved the way for the Early Modern era of warfare.

Submissions

The publishers would be pleased to receive submissions for this series. Please email info@helion.co.uk, or write to Helion & Company Limited, Unit 8 Amherst Business Centre, Budbrooke Road, Warwick, CV34 5WE

You may also be interested in:

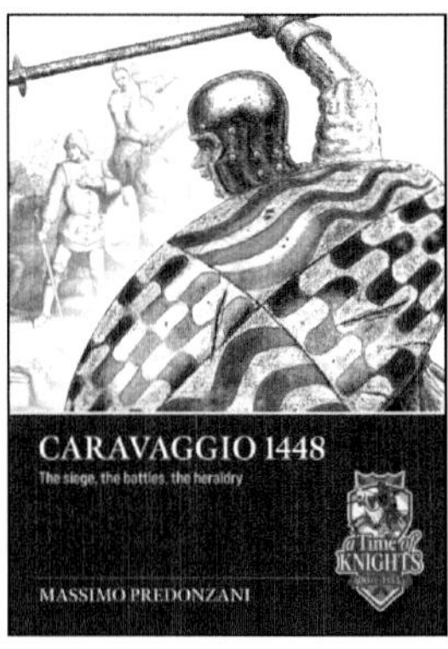

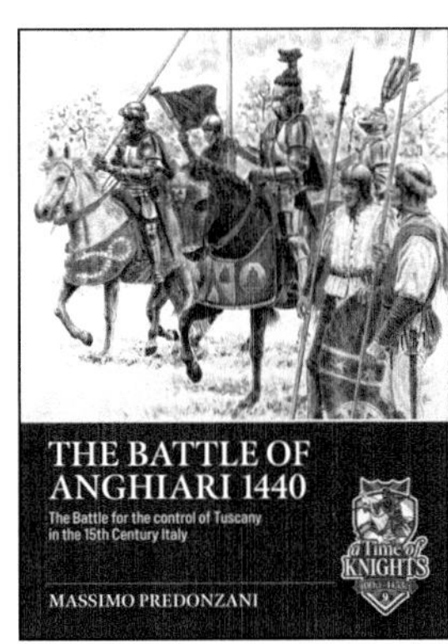